Practical Books for Smart Marketers from PMP

Now you can equip all your sales and marketing people with **Under the Influence**. It will help them introduce new solutions to your existing customers and open the doors for new business development. You may also want to distribute the book to potential customers to help them understand the size and purchasing power of this market and its implications for their industry.

A customized edition, with "*Compliments of* **Your Company Name**" on the cover is available with orders of 200 or more copies.

Call us toll-free at **888-787-8100** for quotes on quantity orders.

For more practical books for smart marketers, go to our website, **www.paramountbooks.com**.

Tracing the Hip-Hop Generation's Impact on
Brands, Sports, and Pop Culture

Erin O. Patton

Paramount Market Publishing, Inc.

Paramount Market Publishing, Inc.
950 Danby Road, Suite 136
Ithaca, NY 14850
www.paramountbooks.com
Telephone: 607-275-8100; 888-787-8100   Facsimile: 607-275-8101

Publisher: James Madden
Editorial Director: Doris Walsh

Cataloging in Publication Data available
ISBN 978-0-9801745-4-0

FOREWORD

In January of 2009 my family and I had the opportunity to serve as hosts for two ten-year-old boys from Korea. Although we could not, and still cannot speak Korean, knew little about their culture, and actually knew even less about the boys themselves, we were excited about having them live with us for a couple of months. When we made the trip to suburban Austin to meet the boys who had just arrived in the United States we had no idea what to expect. To my surprise, one of the boys, "Joey," was dressed like he could have been from the south side of Chicago, the west side of Detroit, the east side of Cleveland, the streets of Brooklyn, or west Philly. He wore a puffy vest, a hoodie, a polo, cuffed baggie jeans, and a pair of 50 Cent G-Unit Reebok knockoffs. Once we got in the car I immediately asked, "Do you listen to hip-hop?" He laughed and said "no." Although his style of dress was clearly influenced by hip-hop fashion, Joey had no idea that he was exhibit A in a revolutionary phenomena: the globalization of hip-hop culture.

As a professor who teaches (along with a colleague) an award-winning course on race, sport, and hip-hop, *Under the Influence*, will help us explain how a ten-year-old boy from Korea, who had never been to the United States, has been influenced by this cultural movement.

Under the Influence is a groundbreaking work for several ways. It is the first book to really look at the hip-hop generation's impact on popular culture, brands, and sports. Throughout the book Erin Patton provides great detail in explaining how the attitude, swagger, and lifestyle of hip-hop moved quickly from the 'hood to Madison

Avenue. As a boy who grew up in suburban Cleveland I remember how we would go to the mall after school and hang out in the polo section of Higbee's, or go to Value City in search of irregular Izods and other designer gear. Further, I remember when my entire crew purchased Timberlands only to wear them unlaced in Cleveland's snowy and bitter winters. Then one day while walking through Saks Fifth Avenue, we noticed that the white mannequin was wearing a polo, hoodie, baggie jeans, and unlaced Timberlands. How ironic. A store that always looked upon us young black males with suspicion was now appropriating our culture and selling it back to us.

This book is also groundbreaking in that it is written by an insider, in fact, someone who has actually been at the forefront of taking urban culture to the mainstream. As the former director of product and marketing for the Jordan Brand, the architect of the Starbury Movement, and as the owner of a firm that has worked with countless Fortune 500 companies, Erin discusses the tactics, strategies, and methods he has utilized in helping hip-hop move from the underground to prominence in the global marketplace. He has been a trailblazer, a visionary, a man ahead of his time. For instance, his innovative 7 Ciphers marketing framework enjoys widespread application in many sectors of industry as it dispelled the myth of a homogenous urban market.

Last, *Under the Influence* is also an inspirational career guide for seasoned professionals and for today's aspiring movers and shakers who want to do things the hip-hop way. Erin personifies the maturation of hip-hop. He takes readers on a journey from his childhood in inner-city Pittsburgh to the boardrooms of corporate giants. While this book is a story about the hip-hop generation's affect on brands, popular culture, and sports, it is also a book about Erin Patton and what one is able to accomplish when they combine the hustle, swagger, and attitude of the hip-hop generation with traditional training.

Erin is hip-hop.

LEONARD N. MOORE
THE UNIVERSITY OF TEXAS AT AUSTIN
JANUARY 2009

PREFACE

From the pimped-out rides we drive, technology we adopt, and brands we wear to the beverages we drink, music we listen to, and language we speak, the Hip-Hop generation has had an intoxicating effect on popular culture and the global economy. In large part, this influence can be traced to members of Generation X who came of age with Hip-Hop music, which came to represent more than just a sound. It became a conduit to self-expression, status, and both political and social awareness.

In the process, out of pure necessity, Hip-Hop innovators applied creativity and ingenuity against the backdrop of the inner city, urban landscape to transform their music and culture into a lifestyle, attitude, and distinct set of brand preferences that would be emulated and adopted by the masses. The music and culture also became an avenue for enterprise as these self-made Hip-Hopreneurs redefined the American Dream.

Understanding this ongoing effect is crucial to success in an increasing range of product categories, from automobiles to consumer electronics, entertainment, fashion, food and drink, mobile phones, sports, entertainment, tourism, and marketing many kinds of luxury and mass merchandise.

Beginning with my own journey from Hip-Hop consumer to Hip-Hop marketer, I explain how Hip-Hop has become a dominant economic force, building brands, and directly or indirectly influencing the aspirations and buying patterns of consumers of all ages. As urban culture has permeated the mainstream, various sub-segments have emerged, each contributing a unique interpretation of the urban culture. These segments transcend race, age and geography and are the new general market. My analysis of these segments is called the 7 Ciphers and you'll learn more about them in Chapter 4.

I examine the yin-yang cultural effect between the Core Urban consumers from the Northeast and the Tertiary Urban consumers from the South who currently have the strongest influence on pop culture.

I also reveal the history behind the fusion of Hip-Hop, skate culture, and rock music, which forms the Alternative Urban Cipher. As a self-professed member of Hip-Hop's Generation X, I detail how this influential group designed the blueprint for modern urban culture, is predisposed toward premium brands, and is the first African-American generation to pass down significant wealth, yet remains one of the most overlooked by marketers. And I show how the influence of these segments reaches across all racial, geographic, and demographic boundaries to America's whitest, most affluent suburbs as well as to consumers in Japan, Europe, and the rest of the world.

Using real-life case studies, illuminating timelines, and profiles of Hip-Hop notables who wield influence from the street corner to the boardroom, I illustrate how urban culture software developers and content creators determine which version of urban culture will run on corporate America's mainframe each year.

These individuals have traditionally used inner-city America as their laboratory. Now global influencers such as Nigo and his A Bathing Ape brand are leveraging the urban mindset they adopted from Western Hip-Hop culture and turning cities like Tokyo into laboratories to manufacture cultural software for export to the United States.

The brands consumers eventually adopt are determined by these innovators and by early adopters in the Hip-Hop community. Awareness of, and demand for, hot new products and styles arise organically and spread virally. As I show through examples like upstart liquor brand Hpnotiq, some companies can manipulate the organic process that occurs within the laboratory of the urban experience and incorporate the Hip-Hop generation's penchant for innovation and savvy insights into product development to ride Hip-Hop's buzz to huge profits, at a fraction of their usual R&D budget. The prospect of participating in this phenomenon has motivated the world's most recognizable and profitable brands like McDonald's, Coca-Cola, and Toyota, to invest significant resources to reach a brand-loyal, savvy, yet often elusive Hip-Hop target.

Companies face a sobering dilemma in trying to measure the effectiveness and ROI of marketing against this target, while battling their own lingering uneasiness about compromising their relationships with traditional consumers in order to reach urban consumers. This uneasiness rests on several misconceptions about today's consumers, and I offer market-tested solutions to guide companies in recognizing distinct brand preferences and attributes that broaden the brand access point to acquire new customers without sacrificing existing customers' loyalty.

ERIN O. PATTON
DALLAS, TEXAS
NOVEMBER 2008

PART 1

Evolution of

I Am

When did I first fall in love with Hip-Hop? It was in 1986 that Hip-Hop's golden arrow hit me as I was waiting for my pre-calculus class period to start at Peabody High School in Pittsburgh, Pennsylvania. In this case, Cupid came in the form of a rapper from Long Island, New York. One of my friends passed me a cassette tape he had just received from his cousin in New York, who was also from "strong island," of a rapper named Rakim. I popped the tape into my Walkman and listened intently to the lyrics of the song called "My Melody." I'll never forget it.

> I'll take 7 MCs put 'em in a line
> And add 7 more brothers that think they can rhyme
> Well it'll take 7 more before I go for mine
> And that's 21 MCs ate up at the same time.
>
> RAKIM, "MY MELODY"

I can't tell you what formulas the calculus teacher talked about that day but Rakim's math was more than sufficient for me. I also loved to express myself through writing so it was inevitable that I started writing my own rhymes.

We would eventually have rap "battles" during lunchtime in the boys' bathroom. I won my fair share and lost a couple, too. From that point on, no matter what, Hip-Hop went wherever I went. LL Cool J's

Radio was the soundtrack for my junior year in 1986 and **Run-DMC**'s *Rock Box* became my workout anthem for summer football practice.

During this time, Hip-Hop also became more than just a sound. Rappers began talking about shoes and clothes and their album covers always showcased the hottest gear. All of a sudden, it became very necessary to wear a Kangol hat because LL Cool J sported one or Adidas shell toes once Run-DMC dropped its classic "My Adidas."

The pressure was on to find a fresh pair of shell toes with the fat laces like the BBoys on the classic Hip-Hop film *Krush Groove*. I was raised in a single-parent household with two older brothers in the tough Homewood-Brushton section of Pittsburgh so things were tight financially for us. Mom worked two jobs just to keep food on the table, and much to my chagrin, shell toes were not a priority over the light bill that month. One day after finishing a baseball game, I found a stack of dollar bills lying in the outfield grass. I dashed to David's Shoes in the East Liberty section of the city, which always had the newest shoes, to get a pair of shell toes. I was disappointed to find the price tag after the tax was more than the $20 in crumpled bills I had.

As I walked back toward the bus stop disheartened, I walked by a store that had what looked like a pair of shell toes. They even had three stripes. Unfortunately, they didn't have the Adidas name. I bought them anyway. The next day in school, I quickly learned the two golden rules of the Hip-Hop culture and lifestyle: Authenticity and Originality.

If you didn't have the latest, you'd be ridiculed. And, boy, did it get tougher and tougher to keep up. The brands moved swiftly from Adidas sneakers to Air Jordans, sweat suits like Le Coq Sportif, and outerwear such as Starter jackets for the guys. Meanwhile, brands like Sassoon and Gloria Vanderbilt became must haves for girls.

Hip-Hop Quotable

I've been in the game for ten years making rap tunes
ever since honeys was wearing Sassoon

Dr. Dre, "California Love"

The thirst for designer wares became insatiable and was born out of a desire to demonstrate to our peers that we were cool. It also gave us a temporary hold on the finer things in life, which were typically beyond our grasp. All of a sudden, this array of fashion and clothing brands, which was being fueled by Hip-Hop's growing imagery and funneled through its clever lyrics, became the canvas for my friends and I to create our own style.

In the summer of 1987, I left Pittsburgh to attend college outside of Chicago at Northwestern University in Evanston, Illinois, and I took Hip-Hop with me.

The period of the late 1980s and early 1990s were clearly the golden years for Hip-Hop music and the onset of the urban mindset in critical mass as well as the early formation of distinct segments within the population. Artists like EPMD (acronym for Erick and Parrish Making Dollars) and Big Daddy Kane, who made gold the jewelry of choice for us, epitomized the fulfillment of the lifestyle aspirations of the Hip-Hop generation to access material trappings.

Conversely, groups like Public Enemy and KRS-One's Boogie Down Productions raised the level of political and social awareness, countering the early consumerism exhibited by the Hip-Hop generation, while De La Soul and A Tribe Called Quest supplanted brand consciousness with self-consciousness and positive self-expression. On the West Coast, N.W.A. brought tales of the streets and gangs to the culture and were one of the first to make sports team apparel popular by donning Los Angeles Raiders (NFL) gear to promote their menacing brand imagery. During this time, apparel brands such as Cross Colours, T.R.O.O.P., and Tommy Hilfiger flourished along with Hip-Hop's rising popularity. In a later chapter I'll discuss how Tommy Hilfiger failed to leverage the loyalty of urban consumers that, ultimately, led to the decline of the brand's pop culture relevance and sales.

When I graduated from Northwestern's Medill School of Journalism in 1991, Hip-Hop's new urban culture was just beginning to plant its seeds within corporate America. I started my career at Burrell Communications Group in Chicago as a public relations intern.

Tom Burrell, one of the early pioneers in African-American advertising, founded Burrell Communications. Burrell was the leading African-American agency during that time and found huge success as companies began to realize the importance of reaching specific, multi-cultural "segments."

Although the Hispanic market was receiving very little attention at the time due to the language barrier, Burrell was making strides by showing companies that African-American consumers spoke English just like the general market but not always the same language, culturally. Jim Hill, a former McDonald's executive, and Michelle Flowers, led the PR arm of Burrell. Jim and Michelle are widely regarded as two of the industry's most prominent African-American PR practitioners.

Burrell had a host of Fortune 500 clients, including Brown-Forman, McDonald's, Coca-Cola, Quaker Oats, and Procter & Gamble. My first assignment was to handle publicity for Procter & Gamble's sponsorship of the six-city Black Family Reunion Celebration, which was the brainchild of the legendary Dr. Dorothy Height of the National Council of Negro Women.

The tour was a great success and enabled Procter & Gamble to connect African-American families with its products, from Tide to Crest and Head & Shoulders. I wrote press releases for each event, coordinated interviews for Procter & Gamble, and distributed photos of the celebrities who participated to local media. I was even able to use my rhyming skills as part of the promotion we did for Procter & Gamble's Sunny Delight brand. We gave visitors to the Sunny Delight booth the chance to rap to Sunny Delight lyrics I penned.

Jim, Michelle, and my boss, Deborah Taylor Lucien, were great mentors for me and were instrumental in convincing me to abandon my plans of being a journalist (and aspiring rapper) for a career in public relations and marketing. I remain grateful to them to this day for placing me in position to leverage my background and urban market insights. It was during that summer that I discovered the unique value of combining my inner-city experience with the skills I'd honed through valuable programs like Inroads. Inroads was founded in the 1980s to help minority students prepare for corporate America and professional success through internships, workshops, and mentoring.

I credit Inroads with much of the success I have experienced today. As an inner-city kid with no corporate role models, I learned how to dress for an interview and navigate the often-turbulent waters of corporate America.

It was also around this time that Burrell forged a revolutionary marriage between Hip-Hop and corporate America with its ads for Sprite featuring rap duo Kid 'n Play. The duo was commercial friendly and their music was positive and youthful.

Kid 'n Play made the hit film *House Party* and embodied the creativity of Hip-Hop's innovators. The duo invented dances, fashions and hairstyles. Kid is best remembered for bringing the "High Top Fade" or Gumby haircut to the masses.

Armed with a solid foundation in multicultural marketing, I left Burrell for a general market public relations agency in Chicago, Edelman Worldwide. As the only African-American account executive in the firm, I leveraged my knowledge of the African-American market to help agency clients such as KFC, Microsoft, and Brown-Forman tap into this growing segment. I'll never forget getting a call from an up-and-coming rap group who had a song called "Southern Comfort," which was one of Brown-Forman's leading brands.

I developed a proposal for a program and partnership with the group to help the brand promote its product and increase trial among African-Americans. While it appears that the program proposal never made it to the client, the group made it into the industry and achieved moderate success. I can only imagine what it might have done for both of them if the memo had made it to the client.

While I quickly gained the favor of Edelman founder and legendary public relations figure Dan Edelman, I learned that I was ahead of my time. After a couple of frustrating years at the agency, I was ready for a change when I received a call from a headhunter asking if I'd be interested in a position with Kellogg in Battle Creek, Michigan.

I visited the Kellogg headquarters in Battle Creek for a round of interviews that I felt went great. Needless to say, I was shocked when the human resources manager called to say they loved me, but had decided to give the job to someone else. As the saying goes, when one door closes, another one opens. It's just the time in between that we spend in the hallway that makes us most uncomfortable. Two weeks later I received another call from the headhunter, this time asking if I'd be interested in working for Nike.

Growing up in inner-city Pittsburgh, I never dreamed of one day living in Oregon, but I agreed to interview. As a three-sport high school letterman that grew up in the City of Champions during the Pittsburgh Steelers and Pittsburgh Pirates dynasties, I felt as if I had died and gone to heaven when I visited Nike's Beaverton campus. I had interviews with head of public relations, Keith Peters and his boss, Donna Gibbs, who was director of corporate communications. Donna became a great mentor for me and would later give me a crash course on crisis communications as Nike faced child labor allegations fueled by Kathie Lee Gifford. Donna took a lot of heat and stood in the face of it.

I was eventually offered the job as manager of public relations. I went from hounding journalists to cover PR stunts to having award-winning journalists like the *New York Times'* Bill Rhoden calling me for official Nike comment.

Shortly after I joined Nike, the PR team hosted a summit on the Nike campus to prepare our athletes for the following summer's Olympic Games. Three weeks into the job I was sitting in a room with the likes of Jackie Joyner Kersee, Carl Lewis, Gail Devers, Sheryl Swoopes, Lisa Leslie, Vlade Divac, and Reggie Miller.

Responsibility for core Nike categories was distributed among several PR managers. I was delegated to look after men's basketball, NCAA, minority affairs, and the company's P.L.A.Y. Program (Participate in the Lives of America's Youth). The P.L.A.Y. program was a cause-related initiative designed to provide youth with a positive outlet to enjoy the benefits of sports and recreation. P.L.A.Y. was especially important to me because I had so recently been one of the kids we were trying to reach. Coming from a tough, inner-city neighborhood, sports played a critical role for my brothers and me and kept us out of trouble. I shared the P.L.A.Y. program's belief that instead of joining a gang, kids should be able to join a team. We refurbished inner-city playgrounds and basketball courts, and provided mentors for kids from disadvantaged backgrounds. The program also provided them with personal contact with an athlete hero who was always on hand for the court dedications.

My first P.L.A.Y. event was at Chicago's Robert Taylor housing project with Chicago Bulls star Scottie Pippen. I remember picking Scottie up in the limo at his home in the Highland Park suburb of Chicago. Like the kids we encountered later that day, I grew up aspiring to be like athletes and here I was up-close and personal with a superstar. Pip and I hit it off and went on to establish a good rapport. Direct contact with the Nike athletes was typically reserved for the sports marketing managers. My relationship with Pip would pay huge dividends during the 1996 Olympics as we created a diary (which was, essentially, a blog) that received a lot of media attention and the favor of my bosses.

My involvement in the P.L.A.Y. program was extremely gratifying. However, nothing would rival my experience in working the men's basketball category.

Date with destiny: Going one-on-one with Michael Jordan

A few short months into the job, I went to Chicago for a Michael Jordan commercial shoot. Basketball was my true love and passion. Like most inner-city kids, I looked up to MJ because of his skills and his style, which made baggy shorts required for all and a bald head desirable even for those without incipient hair loss. In addition, MJ and I were both members of Omega Psi Phi fraternity. I walked into the armory on Chicago's south side and was told I needed to brief him on an interview that we would use to package with behind-the-scenes footage for the launch of the Air Jordan XI.

MJ was true to form. He had a magnetism and approachability that belied his stature. He was engaged in hearty laughter and conversation with the middle-aged Caucasian woman who was the driver of his trailer and, apparently, maker of the best hot chocolate this side of the Mississippi. Having experienced "the Hawk" (wind) in Chicago, I know how a person can covet hot chocolate.

The shoot was a success. I left feeling as if my career had reached a pinnacle. Little did I know it was only the beginning. In the late summer of 1996, I got a call from Peter Ruppe who was the men's basketball category business director (CBD). Peter said Nike was thinking about starting a brand for MJ and the team wanted to know if I would be interested in the marketing position. I agreed to take on the challenge and headed to Tokyo a few weeks later for the Hoop Heroes tour with MJ, Charles Barkley, and Jason Kidd. While I made the trip in my official PR capacity, it was definitely a chemistry check designed to gauge MJ's comfort level with me coming into the Jordan brand role. I recall sitting in MJ's suite with Howard "H" White, MJ's original Nike representative dating back to the early 1980s and among his closest friends, as he seized the opportunity to lightly mention to MJ that they were thinking of having me join the brand. The silence was deafening.

MJ never looked up from the card game and uttered something about Nike handing the keys over to the "new jacks." I didn't know it then, but would later come to appreciate that moment as an example of MJ's masterful approach to both challenge me and signal Howard that he trusted his judgment at the end of the day, but wouldn't hesitate to let him know who made the errant pass if, in fact, I dropped the ball.

Fortunately, Howard was a pretty good floor general. In fact, he was a world-class basketball player himself at the University of Maryland, so much so that his jersey simply carried the letter "H." He was revered at Nike for his unique people skills and uncanny ability to inject life skills into business. A visit to his office was therapeutic. It is little wonder he became such a close confidante to CEO Phil Knight. "H" was also broadly respected in the sports marketing arena and was the gatekeeper to all of Nike's elite athletes. The athletes trusted "H" explicitly and looked to him for sage advice and to act as an honest broker between the often harsh realities of business at Nike and the athlete's individual perspective, needs and grievances in order to fully buy into the process.

Not knowing if I had passed the test was torture, but the Tokyo trip was a great experience. Having later witnessed first-hand the adulation MJ received from fans from all walks of life, I can honestly say nothing compared with the reaction of fans in Japan who would, literally, chase our tour bus on foot for miles. The Air Jordan sneaker and MJ were both cult-like symbols in Japan so the reaction to him descending upon Tokyo appeared to be an out-of-body experience for fashion-crazed teens and the media who made the U.S. paparazzi look like the local photography club. Upon our return back to the states, I flew to Chicago with "H" and Tinker Hatfield, the legendary Air Jordan designer and most creative person I've ever met, to meet with MJ along with the another Nike apparel executive who was to handle the product role for the new brand.

How does one prepare for an interview with the greatest basketball player on the planet? I chose to do a lot of listening, which turned out to be the right decision. It was more of a pep talk and historical perspective on what had become a legendary process of infusing his personality and style into products that became must-haves for inner-city kids like me. While I listened a lot, apparently I said something right on that fall evening at his offices along Chicago's Magnificent Mile, because I became the director of product and marketing for the Jordan brand after my other colleague was unable to leave his current position with Nike apparel.

I spent several months crafting the Jordan brand business plan along with a small nucleus from finance and an internal specialist who assisted in the development of Nike's business units, including the golf division. We eventually presented the plan to Nike president Tom Clarke and the management team. We lobbied management heavily for the resources and support required across the organization to build the business. While many in management were not totally convinced of the viability of creating a separate brand for MJ, we were able to secure the necessary commitments to proceed with the brand launch.

My efforts to get the brand off the ground were supported and made possible by the talented brain trust who helped mine Nike's "crown jewel" Air Jordan franchise through the years: "H," Tinker, Mark Parker, Peter Ruppe, Fred Whitfield, and others including Keith Houlemard, David Bond, and Larry Miller. Miller eventually became the president of the Jordan brand for several years before moving on to a similar post with the NBA's Portland Trailblazers.

For athletes, there are certain moments that justify the blood, sweat, and tears invested and required to achieve greatness. Walking onto the court for the NCAA Final Four, or making the long walk with the lead on the 18th hole are two.

For me, that moment was **the launch of the Jordan brand in 1997 at Niketown in New York.** All of the preparation, long hours, doubts, and internal debates were finally being rewarded. And there was no better backdrop than Niketown.

Nike talks a lot about romancing the brand at retail. Niketown is a shrine to all things consumers love about Nike and sports, not the least of which are its products that are merchandised beautifully on multiple levels along with memorabilia from athletes and interactive kiosks.

Niketown New York is located on Fifth Avenue and 57th Street, which appropriately put us in the center of the fashion universe that day to birth the namesake brand for the ultimate purveyor of style. The launch was celebrity-filled and hosted by MJ's close friend Ahmad Rashad who interviewed MJ, Tinker, and me in a live, roundtable format before we unveiled the new line.

We brought Hip-Hop sensibilities to bear during the launch by incorporating Ed Lover and Dr. Dre of *Yo! MTV Raps* fame as co-hosts and including Hip-Hop group A Tribe Called Quest and R&B group Blackstreet with super-producer Teddy Riley to model the new line in addition to Hollywood friends of MJ such as actor Kadeem Hardison. Media coverage included a front-page story in *USA Today* and wall-to-wall TV coverage from CNN to ESPN.

While some media outlets such as *The Source*, which at the time was the bible of the Hip-Hop industry and urban culture, understood clearly why the Jordan brand was positioned with the urban target and used Hip-Hop as a means to reach the consumer, many in the media and within Nike questioned such a brand positioning for fear of compromising MJ's mainstream image. Indeed, MJ was revered by people from all races and corners of the globe and transcended race like no one else before.

However, I contended that while MJ had achieved a mass appeal, his products held a unique brand positioning and attributes among the core, inner-city kids who might never touch a basketball court but will spend $150 for a new pair of Air Jordans for lifestyle reasons and wear them as a badge of status and self-validation. The shoes and gear were being dropped in Hip-Hop lyrics and being worn in the most popular rap music videos. It didn't take a whole lot of qualitative market research to know this because I was part of that mindset and came from the same place. I also knew that whatever products these urban consumers identified and stamped as cool would be adopted wholesale by suburban kids.

It was cool for Ball Park Franks or Hanes to capitalize on MJ's wholesome image to appeal to the mainstream. However, his Air Jordan franchise was built, in large part, by these inner-city consumers who eventually influenced the white, suburban kids to adopt the hallmarks of their lifestyle. Furthermore, the numbers didn't lie and the sales reps would attest to the fact that urban accounts were significant drivers of sales.

This was still 1997, and while Hip-Hop and urban culture had begun to penetrate the mainstream, corporate America wasn't quite ready yet with the exception of a few brands like Sprite that were actively using Hip-Hop artists such as Grand Puba, Pete Rock, and CL Smooth in their commercials.

As I watched the blanket coverage of the Jordan brand launch that afternoon, I knew corporate America would soon have to adjust to this new order. But I did not yet know just how monumental that shift would be.

Erin Patton (far left) and Michael Jordan receive the Edison Best New Product award from the American Marketing Association.

CHAPTER 2

Diary of an

URBAN CONSUMER SCIENTIST

One of the greatest benefits in working at Nike was its consumer focus. We spent a lot of time in the market as consumer scientists, observing behaviors and market dynamics. If you touched product, you spent most of your time on the road honing in on consumer inspirations and trends because it was pretty difficult to do that from Beaverton, Oregon.

Real-time urban consumer insights and key touch points

The Jordan brand was especially critical because it was Nike's crown jewel and was coveted most by urban consumers. I spent a lot of time keeping my ear to the streets to learn as much as I could about our target consumer and what motivated them. Nike conducted traditional focus groups, but I was fond of creating non-traditional focus group settings on street ball courts and at urban athletic specialty retailers to get an organic feel for the consumer. My bag was always packed with Jordan product that hadn't come out yet, which always made the kids go nuts. "Alpha" consumers were the trendsetters who were leaders among their peers and wanted the product first. Inevitably, they would influence others in their peer group. I spent most of time in New York and along the Northeast corridor where most of the trends started so I could track these consumers.

It was my version of a consumer tracking study. Many of my business decisions surrounding product, advertising, and marketing tactics were instinctive because I knew what was motivating consumers in real-time. I found out why certain sneaker styles played in the South better than the Northeast or why certain colors were hits in the Midwest and on the West Coast.

In New York, one of my favorite reps to travel with was Astor Chambers who *was* New York. Astor would always point me in the right direction and let me know what was happening with the Jordan product and the consumer. We would go uptown to Harlem to 125TH Street and spend time at retailers like Dr. Jays and Jimmy Jazz. This was prior to Old Navy, Starbucks, and others coming in. We'd normally hit the store around 3 p.m. to catch the "sneakerologists" as we called them. The customers were the kids who could tell you more about the sneaker than the product marketer. Like me, Astor was once one of those same alpha consumers so we were able to extract the desired qualitative feedback from the target and I would bring the intelligence back to Portland and the product team so we could stay as close to market as possible.

Many times I would act as a secret shopper and ask the sneakerologists what they liked about the Jordan product they were buying. It was unbelievable how pre-meditated the purchase was. Kids would walk into Dr. Jays, head up the stairs, and go straight to the sales associate without even looking at the shoe wall.

In fact, the only question they asked about the product was if their size was available. The numbers of young girls who purchased the Air Jordan product also amazed me. It wasn't rare on the release day for Air Jordans to spot an entire family sporting the latest version.

Another place I frequented was the Grand Concourse in the Bronx. Literally, store after store for a two-mile stretch could be found selling the latest footwear and apparel. A few hours on the Concourse was enough to learn which sneakers were in, which fashions and colors were hot, and which Hip-Hop artists were about to become future stars.

In Brooklyn, Fulton Street was a major artery and always ripe with fresh urban consumer insights. I could also pick up the latest underground Hip-Hop mixtape. Mixtapes are actually in CD form and are a collection of unreleased songs from Hip-Hop artists. They are sold on street corners and in bodegas, usually for $5 or $10. It was well worth it because they came with 20+ songs and tracks that you would probably never hear played on the radio or get released from the label.

Mixtapes eventually became a power-ful marketing tool that made unknowns like 50 Cent household names on the underground circuit before they got major record deals. They also provided the DJs such as **DJ Clue** who compiled the mix-tapes, a platform to eventually reach the MTV generation. Mixtapes let us hear which artists were mentioning the Jordan  product in their lyrics and I often cited these during sales presentations before eventually producing Jordan brand promotional mixtapes to support footwear product launches.

In Manhattan, Transit in lower Manhattan incorporated a sub way motif into the concept and did a really good job merchandising the product. Transit was a destination retailer and I often conducted impromptu focus groups there with new products we were considering to get aesthetic input on colors and materials.

Along the Northeast corridor, I canvassed the urban markets in Philadelphia, Baltimore, and Washington, D.C., at hot spots like Up Against The Wall. Usually the urban specialty retailers were doing the best with urban products. The national retailers like Foot Locker and Footaction also did their best sales numbers in the inner city.

On the West Coast, Los Angeles wasn't known at the time as cre-ating many trends but it was an important market for Nike and the Jordan brand. It was more difficult for market travel because it didn't have the same density of stores as New York. Like everything else in LA, the locations were spread out.

One of my favorite spots in Los Angeles was Inglewood, home to

Inglewood Sports, a popular urban athletic specialty retailer. I took the latest shoes to Inglewood Sports, often bringing Jordan designers along to give them a feel for the consumer and additional inspiration.

One of our designers, Wilson Smith, had designed most of Andre Agassi's product and had come over to the Jordan brand. One of his first projects was to design the first women's Air Jordan, which was no small task.

I took Wilson to Inglewood Sports and he showed the various shoes to some of the female consumers. At the time the shoe was black and white. The female consumers were insistent that he create the shoe in baby blue. Designers don't budge easily, and I wasn't sure how Wilson would react. A year later, the customers were pleased to see the female Jordan shoe released at Inglewood Sports in baby blue. The shoe sold out instantly.

LA also had a good barbershop scene. The barbershop is an institution in the inner city. Rapper Ice Cube from the highly controversial rap group N.W.A. projected this unique experience onto the big screen with his *Barbershop* television and film franchise.

The barbershop is a place to learn about sex, relationships, music, politics, and current events. It's also a place to get caught up on past issues of *JET Magazine*, the long-standing weekly newsmagazine from Johnson Publishing and sister publication to *Ebony Magazine.* Before there was *US Weekly, JET* was the definitive source for black politics, culture, and gossip. It's also one of the most under-valued and under-used media outlets by advertisers and marketers because of its shelf life and inter-generational appeal. For example, issues are routinely passed from one family to another before eventually landing in the beauty salon and barbershop for patrons to peruse while enduring substantial wait times. Talk about CPM and gross impressions.

Most of these barbers are market trendsetters. Barbers are looked to for advice on hairstyles but are also visual icons for what is hot and what isn't hot. There is tremendous foot traffic at the barbershop, so I knew it would be a great place to expose consumers to Jordan Brand products.

I decided to employ a guerilla tactic and give Air Jordan product to the barbers before they were released in stores. My Nike colleague Damon Haley helped me set up a barbershop blitz. Damon was and continues to be all things grass roots marketing in LA. He is now one of the principals of the Urban Marketing Corporation of America (UMCA), which has been very successful designing and executing programs targeting urban consumers. It's based in large part on a transcultural philosophy and understanding of the urban market that Damon shares as a member of Hip-Hop's Generation X.

The importance of being first

It's important to underscore just how critical a requirement it is for urban consumers to access desirable items before others to cement their standing as trendsetters.

By having a product first, the trendsetter affirms his status. As a result the trendsetter is willing to pay a premium. I was routinely offered cash to buy my Jordan product samples simply because they had yet to be released. In one case, a guy offered $500 for a pair of my Jordan samples that weren't even in his size!

By seeding the product with the barbers first, the word of mouth was the greatest form of advertising we could imagine because everyone wanted to see the newest Jordan, which made the demand even stronger because the product wasn't available in the stores yet. To this day, this notion of limited demand and seeding is the single most important element many brands overlook when targeting the urban market.

Shortly afterwards on a trip to Inglewood to meet with the barbers at my favorite shop across from Inglewood Sports, I happened across another barber shop and noticed Reebok had placed a kiosk there. Imitation is the sincerest form of flattery. A few years later, *The Wall Street Journal* did a story on how barbershops had become a marketing tool for brands, citing my innovation with the Jordan product.

Most of the action in LA took place at the malls with the national retailers like Footaction, the first of the athletic specialty retailers to embrace Hip-Hop and urban culture. It realized that the consumer would buy the Air Jordan but then want one of the urban apparel brands to "hook up" with.

For an urban marketer, the notion of the "hook up" is an important one. Because Nike's apparel was performance-oriented and less lifestyle focused, shoe consumers would purchase urban apparel brands to complete their fashion look. The apparel designers for the urban apparel brands would look at the colors for our new footwear to decide which colors they would introduce that season, realizing the consumer would instantly hook it up with the footwear.

Footaction found great success by merchandising footwear and urban apparel "hook ups" with brands such as FUBU, Enyce, and Rocawear to present the entire lifestyle. Sales went through the roof. Later, I also persuaded urban retailers to merchandise the latest fashion accessory, the mobile phone, which helped Motorola become part of the urban lifestyle.

I always tried to leverage the urban consumer perspective back on the Nike campus and during sales meetings. One year, Astor and I did a man-on-the-street segment from the world-famous Apollo Theater in Harlem and included video from some of our retail visits and consumer interactions. The goal was to expose the organization to a world and urban consumer touch points that were relatively unknown to many at Nike.

Another year, a fictitious barbershop set at a sales meeting demonstrated to the sales force how the Jordan product was as much a fixture in urban lifestyles off the court as it was on the court. While market travel was always an eye-opening experience, there was nothing like witnessing a release day for the Air Jordans. Our key consumers knew the day the shoes were releasing and went to extreme measures to be the first to get them. They would line up before the store opened. It wasn't just the core urban kids, either. Consumers would fly over from Japan and other Asian countries to purchase as many of the new shoes as they could.

In response, the stores had to create policies to limit the purchases. In some cases, there were near riots. We received a lot of feedback from parents and schools who expressed concern over students skipping school in order to get the latest Air Jordans. MJ and I talked about the issue and he really wanted to do something about it.

Eventually, we changed our release dates to Saturdays. MJ took a lot of criticism for his supposed lack of social consciousness. With regard to school attendance and the violence associated with gang members who were targeting innocents who wore Air Jordans in the color of a certain gang, MJ demonstrated real concern and compassion for youth and was vocal and instrumental in the decisions we ultimately made.

I remember getting a call from a *Nightline* producer who wanted to do a story on the extremes that kids were going to, including violence, in order to land a pair of Air Jordans. There was much debate at Nike about whether MJ should appear on the program. My PR background told me it would help quell the fervor if he went on *Nightline.*

I also told him it would send a powerful message to parents and educators that he did care about youth and was not disconnected from the impact his image and the product had on their lives. Nike is certainly not one to succumb to pressure to appease its many critics. There was some internal debate, but he did agree to go on. Both MJ and I were interviewed and appeared on the show. The issue quickly died down.

Without question, the footwear and apparel industries have felt a favorable impact from urban consumers. The market feedback from consumers and retail associates on a release day was more valuable than anything I would ever get in weeks of meetings on Nike's campus.

As part of the perspective I carried back to Beaverton to help the brand stay ahead of the curve, I suggested to MJ and my Nike colleagues that he should consider making an impromptu visit to one of the urban retail locations on an Air Jordan release day. No press, no photo ops. Just MJ mingling with consumers as any CEO should. After all, even though he was retired and no longer playing, it was his brand.

Such a visit would send a buzz and type of word of mouth throughout the neighborhood that advertising could never buy. It would go a long way in increasing his relevance among the urban target.

The feeling around the conference room was that MJ needed to keep a certain mystique and visiting a retailer would compromise that. Many did not understand the value of making such a visit to Harlem.

I placed a picture on the table of a younger MJ surrounded by a group of inner-city kids on a playground during his rookie season. The picture was from one of the early commercial shoots where MJ first struck the Jumpman pose, ball outstretched and legs fully cocked gliding through the air against the Chicago skyline. It was an attempt to remind everyone of the urban constituency from which Air Jordan's popularity originally ascended. Here we were some thirteen years later and MJ had become somewhat disconnected from the urban consumer given his global icon status.

My feeling was that it would be a great way for he and the brand to connect to the culture since he was no longer playing and athletes like Allen Iverson and others with "street cred" were beginning to increase their appeal among urban consumers. Mystique eventually overruled street-level buzz and it was decided not to make the visit. There also was legitimate concern over how other retailers might react since they would all have given their right arm to have MJ visit their store on a release day.

Eventually, MJ did make such a visit. Ironically, Nike later announced plans to open a Jordan brand store in Harlem on the very 125TH Street "laboratory" where I began my clinical observations as an urban consumer scientist.

As I canvassed the urban market for Nike and observed the increasing growth and popularity of Hip-Hop music and urban culture, I began to identify several distinct clusters of consumers forming around the urban mindset. This mindset related to their choices and preferences for language, brands, music, fashion and attitude.

The definition of urban underwent a profound perceptual change in the period from 2001 to 2004 as Hip-Hop culture became widely embraced by the mainstream. Urban marketing was no longer readily dismissed as an afterthought or an off-the-radar tactic and urban consumers were no longer the faithful concubines of corporate America.

The negative stigma often encountered at Nike was finally being removed. I recall holding up a picture of Snoop Dogg sporting Air Jordans in a popular urban magazine in the late 1990s as a signal of the importance of Hip-Hop and urban culture, much to the chagrin of my Nike colleagues around the room.

While I was frustrated at the time, I eventually realized that my Nike colleagues weren't opposed to the urban market for reasons of bias. After all, Nike is a sports company and lifestyle always took an appropriate backseat to performance, enabling the brand to stay focused and avoid cyclical fads and fashion. More than anything, it was a matter of evolution, not revolution. Just as Nike had a Future Vision Research and Design process to develop advanced footwear concepts five years out, I was a futurist looking at the evolving marketplace through a similar lens that revealed what the paradigm would look like.

In January 2000 I decided to leave Nike for New York, the Mecca of Hip-Hop, to rejoin Edelman PR Worldwide as head of the diversity marketing consumer practice at the behest of one of my mentors, CEO Richard Edelman.

Edelman's headquarters were located at 1500 Broadway in Times Square, which gave me an office with a bird's eye view of the famed crystal ball on New Year's Eve 2000 and the realization that the future I predicted was now.

CHAPTER 3

The Best Way to Predict the Future

New York is to urban culture what Silicon Valley is to technology. As the birthplace of Hip-Hop music, it has traditionally served as the epicenter for innovation and inspiration within urban culture. New York's pace and competitive street dynamics also foster creativity, ingenuity, and a hustler's ambition among the urban culture "software developers" to come up with the "killer app" for the culture.

That can be a new artist, a new dance, a new drink, or a new brand. Later I'll discuss the role these urban culture "software developers" play in overall marketing schemes. Much like the Internet start-ups that were born out of and led by a new generation of *avant garde*, "techpreneurs" who were products of the Silicon Valley culture and not classically trained business schools, the "Hip-Hopreneurs" who profited most from the urban marketing boom were the Generation X urban culture "software developers" such as Jay-Z, Sean "Puffy" Combs, Ice Cube, Queen Latifah, Jermaine Dupri, and Master P who married their passion for Hip-Hop music and lifestyle with street-level business instincts.

These artists leveraged their understanding of what drove the culture as former users and consumers. They designed the very "programs and applications" corporate America was profiting from to start their own companies and command more equitable partnerships with the "hardware manufacturers" representing the record companies, fashion brands, television networks, and Hollywood studios.

Thus, instead of adopting an apparel brand, wearing it in their videos and generating huge profits for someone else, they launched "insider" brands like Rocawear and Sean John that provided products that reflected the desired fit and look for the urban consumer. Then they licensed it to retailers for distribution to the masses. The marketing and advertising of these brands was also more reflective of the cultural and lifestyle nuances that corporate America could never replicate.

Of course, Hip-Hop music was the prevailing software in the culture. The urban marketing boom of the late 1990s and early 2000s saw a steady stream of independent record labels launched by these Hip-Hopreneurs who signed lucrative distribution deals with the music industry mainframe to reach a broader, mass market audience such as Bad Boy Records (P. Diddy), Roc-A-Fella (Jay-Z) No Limit Records (Master P), So So Def (Jermaine Dupri), and Death Row Records. Death Row Records founder Suge Knight took the Bill Gates approach by owning all of his label's masters and commanding even greater licensing and publishing fees.

These innovators were, in large part, building off a blueprint established by the godfather of Hip-Hop, Russell Simmons. He pioneered the way from the streets to the boardrooms by turning Def Jam records into a brand portfolio encompassing music, fashion, technology, and TV.

Like Russell, these Hip-Hopreneurs eventually mastered the art of designing their software and content to run across multiple platforms. Their clothing brands showed up in the music videos they began directing and even the movies they wrote, produced, directed and appeared in and they licensed their brands to mobile phones.

HIP-HOP QUOTABLE

Far from a Harvard student,
Just had the balls to do it.
  JAY-Z, "WHAT MORE CAN I SAY"

As a demonstration of the bona fide, measurable impact Hip-Hop culture and these entrepreneurs were making on the economy, in 2003, a *BusinessWeek* cover story examined Hip-Hop's influence on corporate

America and dubbing Russell the CEO of Hip-Hop. In that same article I sounded the alarm for marketers that the urban market had formed a critical mass and was the new mainstream general market.

The floodgates were opened on Madison Avenue as everything Hip-Hop touched was beginning to turn gold. Not only was the Big Apple ripe with opportunity, but also it provided a laboratory for clinical observation of urban consumer behavior that supported my philosophy of applying consumer insights in real-time and helping brands generate products and marketing born out of an authentic consumer experience.

Data from the 2000 Census revealed shifting demographic patterns that were presenting a new set of challenges for marketers who could no longer ignore the growth of multicultural populations in the United States. Our vision for Edelman's Diversity Marketing practice to establish a boutique specialty across a general market agency's U.S. office network was right on time. In addition to work for Fortune 500 clients such as Absolut, Home Depot, Pfizer, and Nissan, my sports marketing experience led to us managing Wrigley's Doublemint on its partnership with Venus and Serena Williams.

My team also handled the And 1 Mixtape Tour in 2001. The And 1 Mixtape Tour was an urban culture phenomenon that married Hip-Hop music and lifestyle with street basketball culture. It can best be described as urban Grass Roots Marketing 101. This four-city tour turned into a national grass roots event and mobile marketing model which expanded the content of these street ball software developers from VHS tapes sold underground in the 'hood, to an ESPN original program, and national sponsorships.

We also handled the upstart And 1 sneaker brand's World Wide Ballin' Tour with NBA superstar Kevin Garnett, which took us to London, Milan, and Madrid. This experience further demonstrated how Hip-Hop and urban culture's global influence was being exported. I had been to London a few times, but I was amazed this time around seeing European kids walking around with the And 1 Mixtape in full Hip-Hop regalia praising And 1 street ball legends like Hot Sauce, A.O., and Headache.

Back home, Hip-Hop music and the urban lifestyle continued to influence a growing multicultural experience and form a "psychographic" mindset that was transcending race. At the same time, it had become painfully obvious that our clients at Edelman were "brain cramping" on multicultural marketing and trying to digest how to reach these vastly different cultural affinity groups, African American, Hispanic, Asian American, and how to prioritize budgets against them.

They got stuck on tactical issues such as reaching Hispanics in English or translating to Spanish language and made the natural leap and false assumption that African Americans could be reached via mainstream media since no translation was required. When it came to Asian-American markets, as my market research professor in business school used to say of organizations lacking a true market-based orientation, they basically said, "We'll just punt and go to lunch." Companies often try to find a common nexus to reach all of their customers and perceive multicultural marketing outreach in large part as more of an altruistic imperative than a business imperative.

As the urban audience grew and became less monolithic and more transcultural, I recognized that it was necessary to decode the urban market through an advanced, strategic approach that elevated the opportunity. It needed to reflect the urban market's influence on the mainstream in a way that evolved beyond the prevailing theme of hitching brands to popular trends or simply "what or who is hot." Urban became *the* buzzword.

The evolution of an urban philosophy

I decided to scratch my entrepreneurial itch in 2002 and launched The Mastermind Group (TMG), a brand management and marketing consulting firm, which would be based in New York.

I based the philosophy of my agency on the Master Mind Group principle Napolean Hill outlines in the book, *Think and Grow Rich*. He found that the most successful businessmen such as Henry Ford and Andrew Carnegie attributed their success to surrounding themselves with a Master Mind Group, which allowed them to "coordinate knowledge and effort toward a definitive purpose" and also tap into what he called the "infinite storehouse of intelligence."

This philosophy resonated with me so my business model was to do just that on behalf of clients seeking to reach this influential urban audience. Stedman Graham is a great motivator and talks about understanding your inherent value in pursuit of your life's brand. My value was in my ability to intuitively understand the behavior of urban consumers as a product of the Hip-Hop generation and think forward and strategically about how to coordinate the knowledge and effort required to design a program that would solve a client's problem or give their competitors one to solve.

In other words, once the "urban culture software" is developed, someone has to know how to write the program in a language the hardware mainframe can understand.

At about this time I was invited to address the annual MOBE (Marketing Opportunities in Business and Entertainment) Conference run by Yvette Moyo and her son Rael Jackson. The conference theme was "Targeting the Urban Demo to Build Lifetime Customers," and I posed the question "What is Urban?" In America's consumer-driven matrix, this was a $300 billion question. I concluded that urban was no longer a demographic, but had become a psychographic, a mindset shaped by the cultural phenomenon born in the 1970s called Hip-Hop. I wanted to dispel the myth and false perception in corporate America and society that the urban market equals African Americans. African Americans are a racial, demographic group. Urban is a mindset.

Hip-Hop philosopher KRS-One said that Hip-Hop is an attitude, an awareness, and a way to view the world. From Beijing to the Bronx. From street ball courts in the inner city to skate parks in the suburbs.

On at least three or four radio stations in every major city, urban had become the chosen format for the current generation, which were not just black listeners. However, given that the music and art form was born out of the urban environment, "urban" had pretty much come to be inextricably linked to Hip-Hop and the inner-city black experience. The term had come to represent a fairly narrow perception and conjured up certain stereotypes in the minds of the main-stream.

The mainstream powers, notwithstanding the entertainment indus-try and a few select brands, weren't receptive to tuning into a frequency they could not understand and thought would be confined to a fad. Urban was undesirable to most of the mainstream palate whose taste buds found its flavor a bit spicy. However, a few successful insider brands continued to develop recipes with urban as the main ingredient.

Fast forward to today. Urban culture is extremely desirable to the degree that 50 Cent has moved from underground artist at the start of the century to a debut album in 2003, *Get Rich or Die Trying* that set the record for the most played single in the history of music. He has amassed a fortune and a brand empire that now encompasses his core businesses of music and fashion in addition to revenue streams from movies, videogames, ringtones, a signature deodorant, and fla-vored water.

According to *Fortune* magazine, he pulled in $150 million in pretax in 2007. Much of that 2007 windfall came when 50 Cent made $100 million from his stake in VitaminWater parent Glaceau when it was sold to Coca-Cola.

Jay-Z has lyrically hailed his intuitive ability to predict the future "like Cleo the psychic," but not even he could have predicted he would be able to go from self-professed street hustler to President & CEO of Def Jam records. He oversees a portfolio of brands that landed him at Number 7 on the 2008 *Fortune* Magazine Celebrity 100 list. In addition to music, clothing, and his posh sports lounge 40/40, Jay-Z negotiated a landmark deal with LiveNation for $300 million, which also underscored the value of an urban mass-market audience.

So why is "urban" all of a sudden so desirable to corporate Amer-ica? In addition to the obvious economic benefits, the answer can be traced to what is taking place in America on a macro level. In short, urban is desirable because urban is no longer just black. Urban has been revitalized for mainstream consumption. In places like Chicago, housing projects such as the Robert Taylor Homes and Cabrini Green have been torn down and replaced by lavish town houses, condominiums, and shops. The same thing is happening in Harlem and cities throughout the country.

Furthermore, whereas poor inner-city blacks are being displaced to the southern outskirts of Chicago, the wealthy of all races are migrating back to the city center from the saturated suburban areas. The migration is being supported with commercial and residential investment, not to mention the cultural and entertainment benefits that come with being located at the city's center where all of the activity is taking place.

Cities such as Los Angeles and Dallas are revitalizing once-depressed areas with retail developments, shopping villages, high-end boutiques and luxury residences now being marketed as "urban lifestyle."

Likewise, given the popularity of urban culture, mainstream marketers are now eager to build their brand home in the urban zip code where the marketing action is. In essence, the perception of what "urban" is has changed. And that is both a good thing and an evolution that was inevitable given the growing impact of urban culture on this current generation.

What is urban?

Urban is young. Urban is mature. Urban is multicultural. Urban is multiracial. Urban is classic. Urban is contemporary. Urban is grimy. Urban is luxury. Urban is suburban. Urban is "so hood" as DJ Khaled from Miami boasted in his 2007 anthem. Urban is 50 Cent. Urban is Eminem.

Urban is a "psychographic" not a demographic. Urban is a mindset, based on shared lifestyle interests, not race alone, especially among this generation of youth. Urban is . . . not just black anymore.

On the one hand, this paradigm shift is a good thing, as African Americans have been fighting stereotypical images and monolithic perceptions associated with urban culture in mass media and advertising for a long time. Just as urban culture has evolved, African Americans have also evolved into a broad tapestry of experiences and perspectives, albeit woven with common threads.

There are a multitude of inspirations and expressions within the culture that appeal to its broader sensibilities. As such, it takes more than a Hip-Hop jingle to get African Americans to purchase a brand. At the same time, African Americans want long overdue credit for the creativity and innovation they have contributed to pop culture.

On the other hand, it requires that African-American marketers, media, advertising agencies and the broader community assume a leadership position in defining this new mainstream for their constituents and clients. Given the influence of urban culture as the driver of popular culture, many outside of the culture will be actively engaged in marketing and distributing it, which means the competition will be even greater.

It also means the culture will be subject to "urbansploitation" stereotypes and other pitfalls by mainstream marketers which I'll address in a later chapter. While urban does transcend race, make no mistake, the African-American and Latino urban experience will continue to set the pace for this current generation of change, popular culture, and the global economy.

Arguably, African Americans are among the most creative and innovative population on the planet and are the engine driving mainstream urban culture. This is a combined force of their DNA and their experience of having to "make a way out of no way" and predict their own future by creating it. What African Americans have contributed to the urban market and broader pop culture is the notion of reinvention as a necessary mode of survival. As a result, urban consumers are constantly reinventing themselves and the world around them.

With a flurry of such innovation and reinvention in the 1990s combined with a refinement of tastes and realized aspirations, Hip-Hop's Generation X transformed popular culture in a profound way.

Around this same time, I began to detect different segments coalescing around this urban mindset and current generation, which transcended race, age, and gender. For the first time in our nation's history, a new generation was emerging without racial boundaries. They were identified less by racial differences and more by their common interests that would eventually propel Barack Obama, who embodies this very notion, to become the first African American to be elected President of the United States.

Obama also took a page from Hip-Hop's Generation X audience by making a way from no way and creating a new future with an insurgency campaign built on a platform of change and transcendence. Obama gave a not-so-subtle nod to the origins of this notion within Hip-Hop's Generation X as he mimicked a wiping gesture taken from Jay-Z's song "Dirt Off Your Shoulders" during a press conference after staging an impressive primary victory and facing an onslaught of negative attacks from Hillary Clinton.

Beyond the Benetton utopia of years past, this new paradigm was based on a very real set of experiences and cultural exchanges enhanced by digital technology and delivered through music, podcasts, blogs, and other interactive, multi-media platforms connecting Hip-Hop and urban culture throughout the global village in ways never imagined.

This new paradigm has fundamentally changed the way brands are being forced to market to the current generation. The traditional race-based approach is no longer effective. This new paradigm requires a psychographic approach and segmentation that addresses the nuances within various urban segments to create a customized brand experience for specific audiences.

What has been lacking is a framework for this new paradigm. After spending years studying the urban consumer behavior and market dynamics, I emerged from the lab convinced I had found the solution. Adopting a relevant term in Hip-Hop vernacular I called the segments the 7 Ciphers:

Core Urban

Tertiary Urban

Sub-Urban

Contemporary Urban

Alternative Urban

Vintage Urban

Organic Urban

PART 2

Profit-Coding the New

MARKET TRENDS, MINDSETS, AND BEHAVIORS

CHAPTER 4

The

7 CIPHERS™

Webster's Dictionary defines a cipher as: "*n.* A cryptographic system in which units are arbitrarily transposed or substituted according to a predetermined key. The key to such a system. To put into secret writing or a message in cipher. A design combining or interweaving letters or initials."

In this case, the system is the global marketplace and the units are the teens and various consumer actors who have adopted an urban mindset. The designs combining or interweaving letters or initials are the various sub-segments, which have formed as a result of the proliferation of Hip-Hop culture and lifestyle. The goal for marketers is to decode the ciphers to determine the right message to communicate with them.

This phenomenon reminds me of a scene from one of my favorite movies, *A Beautiful Mind*, with Russell Crowe, where the genius mathematician John Nash is called to the Pentagon to decode a secret cipher to thwart the plans of a group planning to attack the United States. I suggest that the same thing is happening with the urban market. Instead of the Pentagon, the suits are corporate America's brand managers.

Brand managers in an ever-widening array of companies are asking themselves the same questions:

- **What is the size of this market?**
- **How do we quantify it?**

- How do we reach the urban market in a strategic fashion without compromising our core audience?

- How do we identify what and where the next trends are going to be?

- How do we communicate our brand language in a way the urban consumer understands without being too patronizing?

- What is the best way to approach the urban market?

- Who is doing the best job of it?

- Is this a strategy or a tactic?

- Why is this happening to our brand?

The 7 Ciphers offers a framework that allows marketers to crack that code. It also helps parents understand why their kids say they got a little "crunk" last night or they must have the newest flavor of Ice Cream that just released and which may set them back financially a bit. In this case, a trip to Ben & Jerry's won't suffice. To get the Ice Cream these teens want, they will have to buy a pair of the sneakers in super-producer Pharell Williams' Billionaire Boys Club and Ice Cream lines which are targeted to the suburban skate kids who also love rap-rock music.

Within Hip-Hop culture, a cipher has significant historical relevance. Many rappers who were members of the Five Percent Nation, a Muslim sect that gained an immense following in New York, adopted the term cipher. The movement and term made its way into Hip-Hop vernacular in the early 1990s by Hip-Hop artists like Poor Righteous Teachers and Brand Nubian.

For the Five Percent Nation, a cipher was a circular formation of individuals who represented 360 degrees of knowledge. Each individual shared knowledge with the others, each person adding to what the previous person said. In Hip-Hop, a cipher is a circle of individuals who take turns rhyming, with each person building off what the previous rapper says.

In Hip-Hop's most recent vernacular, a cipher also represents an individual's total self-expression. In a lifestyle sense, a cipher represents those elements that make the person unique. For example, particular brands of sneaker, apparel, cell phone, and car can make up your individual cipher.

On a macro-level, within the urban culture, the same thing has happened. A core, inner-city urban experience and influence is adopted but interpreted slightly differently in the suburbs. In tertiary markets such as Atlanta, Houston, Dallas, and New Orleans, there is a southern expression of urban culture, which is manifested in a slightly different lifestyle and expressed through distinct language and brand preferences. This dynamic continues through various other sub-segments such as rap-rock fusion, urban intelligentsia, and globally in places like Japan and Europe. These segments have formed a new general market population of 100 million with $300 billion in buying power according to our 7 Ciphers quantitative study on the urban market, which was sponsored by Pepsi and the Brookings Institution. The significance for this generation is in how their indoctrination occurs.

Each of these segments has adopted its own interpretation of urban and added a twist that makes it unique. Generic marketing messages and advertising will no longer work for this generation that is equally savvy and cynical. In order to be successful, marketers have to recognize the segments that align best against their brand and products and develop marketing messages that are written in the code of those specific ciphers. Let's dig a little deeper and define the 7 Ciphers.

Core Urban—The Innovators

The Core Urban consumers are the innovators and "software developers" I mentioned earlier. These consumers are primarily African-American and Hispanic aged 14 to 25, and live in the inner city. The epicenter for urban culture and much of what becomes adopted by the mainstream popular culture rests with the Core Urban consumers who have traditionally driven trends around music, language, and fashion. Geographically, this consumer can be found living in cities like New York, Philadelphia, Washington, D.C., Baltimore, and Boston.

Reebok clearly recognized the value of the Core Urban consumer and the role Hip-Hop plays with their target when it developed a con-

troversial campaign featuring **the rapper 50 Cent** in 2005. The campaign was called "I Am What I Am." In the commercial, a voice over of a police dispatch call describes a shooting while a voice counts to 9, signifying the number of times 50 Cent was shot. 50 Cent embodies the Core Urban consumer. 50 Cent was raised in Queens, New York, and quickly became involved in a life of crime. He was subsequently shot nine times and developed mythical status in his neighborhood.

50 Cent also represents the influence of the Core Urban consumer on the mainstream. He didn't sell seven million records to kids in the inner city. He sold them to suburban kids, which Reebok also factored into its analysis of its partnership with the artist. If you were to go to a given mall in the suburbs at the height of 50 Cent's rise, chances are you would see a white kid sporting the type of doo-rag that 50 Cent does, a polyester cap worn by African Americans to facilitate a wavy hair style and project a hardcore, street image.

More on this type of suburban adoption of Core Urban trends when we discuss the Sub-Urban cipher. Without question, Core Urban consumers are brand creators who impact products in virtually every industry with innovation and a distinct set of brand attributes to satisfy their own lifestyle preferences. For example, Core Urban consumers took creative license to alter the Timberland boots brand positioning from that exclusively representing outdoor enthusiasts to become the official brand of choice for the rugged, inner-city landscape and signal urban male machismo.

While industries such as footwear and apparel have long benefited from such loyalty and innovation, industries such as automotive are now putting Hip-Hop artists and Core Urban innovators in the driver's seat of their advertising campaigns and new product launches. General Motors now offers standard trucks with 26-inch rims and both the Chrysler 300 and Dodge Magnum created fully "tricked out" 2005 DUB Edition models in collaboration with *DUB* magazine, the bible for the automotive industry. Marketers trying to reach the Core Urban audience really have to look no further than the *DUB* car show tour.

Latino Core Urban consumers from Los Angeles have been the traditional innovators in this category while the African-American rappers and athletes glorified the automotive culture and made it popular with the mainstream. It began with MTV's show *Cribs* which ended each segment with a celebrity showing off his rides, all of which were tricked out with chrome rims, video screens in the headrests, designer interiors, and booming systems.

MTV eventually created a spin-off of *Cribs* called *Whips* and fully jumped in the fast lane of the urban automotive craze with *Pimp My Ride*, hosted by rapper Xzibit who undoubtedly grew up enamored with the urban car culture in Los Angeles.

There was additional creative fusion and innovation to come from Latino and African-American Core Urban culture through the development of the music form Reggaeton—a Spanish-language genre of Dancehall with distinct Hip-Hop and pop-music influences, originating in Panama.

Reggaeton became extremely popular after the new millennium and burst on the scene just as the U. S. Census revealed explosive growth in the Latino population. It was found in heavy rotation on pop-music radio formats, in dance clubs, and blasting from stereos in the suburbs. The new music form's popularity is attributed to **Daddy Yankee, a well-respected Latino artist** who has been around for years.

In 2004, Daddy Yankee teamed up with New York rapper Noreaga, who had already created a loyal following among Core Urban listeners, and released the hit single "Stand Up" which became the anthem for Reggaeton. This marriage with Hip-Hop opened up the Reggaeton market to the mainstream.

As it relates to music, Core Urban consumers were the first to abandon the retail CD format in favor of the mixtape CDs discussed earlier. Mixtapes became a powerful marketing and promotional tool for record labels and artists because it provided them with the opportunity to build a grass roots following among Core Urban consumers. Mixtapes eventually became big business for independent mixtape producers, which led to an industry crackdown and massive raid in 2007 on the offices of DJ Drama in Atlanta. Officers confiscated more than 81,000 mixtape CDs and arrested the popular mixtape DJ.

Cornerstone Promotions is a music-branding agency in New York that successfully constructed its business model around connecting underground Hip-Hop music with brands, eventually facilitating deals between Hip-Hop artists and corporate America to reach the Core Urban audience.

My favorite example of this is a DJ Premier track "Classic," featuring Rakim, Kanye West, and KRS-One, which was an anthem for Nike's Air Force One sneaker. It didn't receive radio airplay, but it was an underground hit on mixtapes and YouTube.

If artists are able to develop a fan base and street credibility on the mixtape circuit, they are bringing an established fan base to the record label. We talked about the success of 50 Cent. Before 50 Cent made it to MTV, he earned his stripes and created a mythical aura on the mixtape circuit by challenging other rappers. The demand for 50 Cent became so great that the risk for the labels was minimized as he had already established a following. It's the street version of American Idol.

In terms of sports, Core Urban consumers are all about basketball. This isn't surprising considering the fact that most of the NBA's players come from the inner cities of America. This created perception problems for the NBA in the late 1990s as it was transitioning from the polished image attributed to Michael Jordan and adjusting to the influx of Core Urban players coming straight out of high school and the inner city. While the NBA is important to Core Urban Consumers, street ball is one of the nuances unique to this cipher. It gave rise to a small sneaker brand in Paoli, Pennsylvania, called And 1, which tapped into the attitude of Core Urban consumers with its brand positioning and grass roots marketing approach. I'll discuss the Hip-Hop generation's impact on sports further in Chapter 8.

Another important nuance for Core Urban consumers is "street cred," which has become a true marketing buzzword. For these youth, it is important to identify with a particular borough, city, or neighborhood, which is part of their individual cipher. A particular geographical location validates them and gives them authenticity. If you watch BET's popular music program *106 & Park* which targets this audience, you'll notice one of the first questions the hosts ask audience members is, "Where are you from?" This provides the opportunity to "represent," a term which eventually worked its way into mainstream lexicon and the likes of Paris Hilton.

Given the mainstream popularity of **Southern Hip-Hop artists like Lil' Wayne,** Outkast, Ludacris, T.I., Nelly, Lil' Jon and the crunk music movement from Atlanta, innovation in urban culture has shifted from the Northeast to tertiary markets in Atlanta, St. Louis, New Orleans, and Houston that once had minor relevance in urban culture, but now command the majority of it. For example, it was once rare to hear a southern artist on the play list on urban radio in the Northeast, but that has changed drastically. Southern artists are now in heavy rotation on urban formats and dominate the pop charts. As a result, a new urban segment and market force has emerged from the New South.

Tertiary Urban—Cool to be country, cool to talk country

Tertiary Urban consumers hail primarily from the Southern United States. These consumers are primarily African American, with a growing share of Caucasians and Hispanics. They can be found in cities and rural areas surrounding hotbeds such as Atlanta (and the surrounding region), Houston, Dallas, New Orleans, Memphis, and Miami. In addition, there is a strong concentration of this segment in Midwestern markets such as St. Louis and Chicago that have a strong Tertiary Urban influence given migration patterns of African Americans from the South to those industrial cities.

I chose the name Tertiary because, historically, consumers in these once secondary markets were not the primary source of innovation and would mostly adopt the urban trends, brand preferences, and lifestyle that emanated from the Core Urban consumer in the Northeast. That said, southern culture always had its own unique expression and tended to hold fast to its own customs, particularly the southern dialect as well as inter-generational cultural institutions such as the Historically Black College and University (HBCU) experience. Because of this, these tertiary markets were not priority markets for most marketers seeking to reach the critical masses within the urban market because the influence was regional and the consumers were primarily late adopters. For instance, at Nike we could track the end of the useful life of a certain footwear style once consumers in certain markets in the South adopted it.

Brands that made their living from urban consumers learned this lesson more painfully. Long after apparel brand FUBU had become passé among the Core Urban consumers in the Northeast, you could find consumers in the malls in the southern region sporting FUBU. In some cases, those individuals were blue-collar adults well outside the core teen fashion target market range for FUBU. This became a clear signal the brand had lost its urban cachet.

The dynamics began to change in the late 1990s and early 2000s with the mainstream success of the group Outkast and the commercial birth of a new movement in the South which was labeled and packaged with a new moniker: The Dirty South. This movement was personified by Percy Miller, a street smart entrepreneur from New Orleans who went by the stage name of Master P. He started his No Limit records empire by selling CDs out of his trunk. No Limit was more than just a name for his record label; it became a brand unto itself.

Miller parlayed his success in Hip-Hop to TV, film, clothing, sports management and earned the dubious distinction of forging Hip-Hop's first father and son duo with the launch of his son Lil' Romeo's music career and Nickelodeon stardom. While Hip-Hop had long-standing roots in the South, the commercial voice of the South finally came through loud and clear in 2003 and 2004. The sound was "crunk," which was an offshoot of the "crumping" style of dancing, and the mouthpiece was Atlanta producer Lil' Jon.

Lil' Jon was a DJ who helped propagate the crunk style of music that developed in Atlanta's nightclubs. Lil' Jon and the Eastside Boys became the self-proclaimed "Kings of Crunk" and took the energy of crunk music into the mainstream. The success of Lil' Jon and the Eastside Boys paled in comparison with Lil' Jon's collaboration with R&B sensation Usher to produce the song "Yeah" which won the Grammy for record of the year. Usher catapulted to the top of the Billboard charts. Corporate America took notice. To coincide with Usher's 2004 tour, Visa issued an Usher debit card and he later introduced a signature fragrance in partnership with Macy's. These forces conspired to make Atlanta the new laboratory for urban culture, eclipsing the Core Urban segment for primary influence over the culture and mainstream, and producing a yin-yang effect between the two. Hip-Hop artist Ludacris picked up the mantle for Atlanta and carried it brashly to Corporate America. Ludacris was also instrumental in popularizing the Cadillac Escalade on his song "Throw Them Bows." His bold proclamation helped establish the Escalade as the SUV of choice for the urban market and helped GM resurrect its Cadillac brand and increase market share over the Lincoln Navigator that previously enjoyed a first-mover advantage among the urban elite but failed to leverage it for fear of distancing its core customers.

Hip-Hop Quotable

Cadillac Grills, Cadillac Wheels
Check out the oil by Cadillac spills

Ludacris, "Throw Them Bows"

While Ludacris didn't receive compensation for his Escalade lyrical endorsement, he would cash in with a lucrative deal with Pepsi who wanted to tap into the growing influence of the southern culture. Shortly after the company announced the partnership, though, Fox News host Bill O'Reilly condemned the company for the relationship, citing Ludacris' misogynistic lyrics and lack of moral values.

The controversy swirled and Pepsi swiftly terminated the relationship with Ludacris.

Pepsi's decision to walk away from Ludacris demonstrated the heightened sensibilities of formalizing relationships with Hip-Hop artists and the importance of approaching the urban market in a strategic fashion with the appropriate level of understanding for the culture. I discuss this notion in more depth in a later chapter on the pitfalls for Madison Avenue in targeting the urban market.

Following Master P's entrepreneurial trail out of New Orleans' Magnolia housing projects was the group Cash Money who will forever be credited with one of Hip-Hop culture's most significant contributions to pop culture lexicon, coining the term "bling bling" to describe their shiny chrome wheels and diamonds.

The southern dialect, once shunned within urban culture, became widely embraced as this segment grew in size and influence. As Master P said, Tertiary Urban consumers in the south "make it cool to be country and use country grammar."

For Tertiary Urban consumers it's all about regional differences in taste from music and language to clothing. Once wholesale adopters of brands stamped by their northern Hip-Hop brethren, they eventually created their own to join the growing list of fashion Hip-Hopreneurs such as rapper Nelly did with Vokal and Apple Bottoms. Even brands born out of New York's Hip-Hop lifestyle recognized the growing influence of Tertiary Urban consumer innovators such as P. Diddy, who eventually tapped Nelly to be the face of his Sean John line.

HBCUs help connect with the Tertiary Urban audience

In addition to the nuances in styles of music, clothing, and language, when it comes to sports, Black college football classics and homecomings are excellent vehicles to reach Tertiary Urban consumers given the heritage of Historically Black Colleges and Universities (HBCUs) in the South. In my opinion, Black colleges are grossly underused as marketing vehicles. Beyond the young adult audience, they provide an intergenerational pipeline into much of the African-American middle class. Some of the nation's most successful entrepreneurs and executives were educated at HBCUs and have achieved very favorable socioeconomic status. In addition, due to the number of events, active social scene, and alumni network, Black colleges are ripe for lifestyle marketing and direct marketing campaigns targeting Tertiary Urban consumers whose lifestyle mindset centers on event occasions.

Finally, HBCUs also provide one of the best cause-related marketing platforms I've encountered as a marketer. A few years ago, I counseled Atlanta-based Internet service provider Earthlink to refine its brand positioning and strategy to go after the Tertiary Urban audience as a primary market for its dial-up services.

It had previously been targeting Northeast markets and placing its ads in magazines like *Essence* and *Black Enterprise.* This strategy was flawed because the more contemporary urban adults reading those magazines were migrating to broadband.

Meanwhile, Tertiary Urban consumers in the south were a fertile ground for dialup because the broadband infrastructure and penetration in the south lagged behind the Northeast. This was particularly true on Black college campuses, a place where the United Negro College Fund (UNCF) was eager to eradicate the digital divide.

Our agency recommended a partnership between Earthlink and UNCF to support the UNCF's technology enhancement campaign. In the process, Earthlink would gain affinity and access to Black college students who were also the chief technology officers (CTOs) in their homes and would eventually persuade mom and dad to switch to Earthlink (and migrate to its broadband service).

Given the importance for this audience to stay connected to friends, family fraternities, sororities, and professional groups, we created a creative platform of "Link Up," which was popular vernacular among urban consumers at the time. Before LinkedIn became the pre-eminent Internet networking tool, urban consumers and particularly African Americans embedded "link up" into their daily terminology with each other to foster networking and business relationships.

We also served up a partnership with critically acclaimed artist India.Arie which was a great match for the brand given her universal appeal, positive image, and grasp on technology. She also attended college in a tertiary market, Savannah, Georgia.

Most consultants and agencies can relate to the phenomenon of holding the perfect prescription for a client who says his head is hurting but doesn't recognize the Tylenol or Excedrin when you hand it to him and, instead, reverts to the same bottle of Nyquil he's been using to get rid of his headache.

Such was my experience with Earthlink. It is a perfect example of a brand that had a first-mover advantage and captive audience with urban consumers who were its primary market, but it failed to realize it. As a result, it prioritized its spending against the "general market," which was less likely to switch from established dial-up competitors such as AOL or emerging broadband giant Verizon.

It also made a series of strategic blunders in its targeting of the urban market through direct mail and other vehicles that not only rendered the brand ineffective in the urban market but led to the demise of the business.

This Earthlink example also underscores an important feature and benefit of the 7 Ciphers. Because the segmentation framework represents a psychographic and mindset there is overlap between the segments. This element is critical as it enables the segmentation to deliver critical mass across segments or function as a niche audience tool for brands wishing to hone in on one particular segment.

In the case of Earthlink, we tapped into the overlap between the Tertiary Urban and Organic Urban segments. Most of the members of the Organic Urban segment, which I'll discuss later in this chapter, are Tertiary Urban consumers who grew up in the South and went on to attend HBCUs or other universities, becoming part of the "urban intelligentsia" as they matured and evolved.

Sub-Urban Cipher—The Eminem factor

The Sub-Urban includes suburban teens and young adults aged 14 to 25 who aspire to replicate the lifestyle experience of the Core Urban consumer. This segment is primarily Caucasian but includes a significant population of African Americans and Asian Americans. Most people outside of the music industry and suburban parents would be surprised to know that more than half of all Hip-Hop CDs are purchased by white, suburban kids.

Rapper Eminem, as depicted in the movie *8 Mile*, best exemplifies the Sub Urban cipher. Eminem, who had aspirations of becoming a Hip-Hop artist, had to immerse himself directly in the culture by crossing over Detroit's 8 Mile Road to test his skills against MCs in the 'hood.

The majority of Sub-Urban consumers adopt trends—primarily language and fashion—that come out of the Core Urban and Tertiary Urban segments. They want to buy into the lifestyle, and they have the disposable incomes to do so.

Thanks to MTV and the Internet, suburban kids now have 24/7 access to urban culture. MTV wisely recognized the growing influence of Hip-Hop on the mainstream by segmenting its brand with MTV2. MTV2 appeals to the suburban teens that are of this urban mindset, in addition to attracting a broader urban audience. MTV's role in the global spread of Hip-Hop shouldn't be understated. *Yo! MTV Raps* was largely responsible for introducing Hip-Hop to the suburban audience.

When asked what he was listening to on his iPod before his record-setting races, 2008 U.S. Olympic hero Michael Phelps boasted rappers Lil' Wayne and Young Jeezy got his mind right for competition (ironically, both of these artists represent the Tertiary Urban segment, reinforcing my earlier point about its growing command on music and pop culture). As mentioned, the Sub-Urban cipher is not just about Caucasian kids. African-American kids from the suburbs who visit relatives in the inner city on a fairly regular basis transport the urban culture from the 'hood to the 'burbs. It's no secret that these continue to be among the most popular kids in high school.

The transporting of urban culture to the suburbs also extends beyond media into retail. Nike's most significant retail partner is Foot Locker Inc., which has broad distribution. Foot Locker has also been responsible for translating the Hip-Hop lifestyle in the suburbs because it has stores in nearly every mall in America. In places like Livonia, Michigan, where 96 percent of its 100,545 residents are white, making it the nation's whitest city according to the 2000 Census, one can find Hip-Hop videos playing on screens at the store's entrance.

A Foot Locker official explained the phenomenon to *New York Newsday* in 2004: "The rapper, the athlete, today they are the buying influencer," said Rubin Hanan, Foot Locker's senior vice president of retail brand marketing. "They are really ingrained in the product. They wear it. They sing about it. It's been very successful."

In addition, retailers such as Marshall's routinely fill their stores with Hip-Hop clothing in predominantly white, suburban areas. "Suburban kids really idolize rappers such as Nelly and Snoop Dogg," says Jenn DeBarge-Goonan, spokeswoman for Marshall's department stores. For proof, all they need to do is check Shannon Raymond's closet. The 15-year-old student from West Islip tries to stay outfitted in Jay-Z's Rocawear, Russell Simmons' Baby Phat, and Hip-Hop staple Ecko.

"Hip-Hop basically tells the truth, the life stories of the people who sing it," said Raymond, adding that the walls of her room are covered with posters of her favorite rappers—Jay-Z, Eminem, Ludacris and DMX. Foot Locker's Hanan said that the days of marketing Hip-Hop-influenced clothes and shoes only to African Americans or even city-dwellers are over.

"It's not color-dependent," he said. "It's about reaching those in urban areas and those who relate to urban style in the culture. Hip-Hop transcends urban and suburban. It's not just one demographic."

Struggling retailer Sears was also betting on Hip-Hop's Sub-Urban effect as it partnered with **rapper LL Cool J** in 2008 on a signature apparel line to help stimulate lagging sales. One of the initial ads in the campaign featured LL Cool J visiting a suburban white family to give a fashion makeover to the kids, with mom even hoping to score cool points by giving LL a fist jab.

There are clear nuances within the Sub-Urban cipher. While these particular consumers gravitate toward Hip-Hop music and urban fashion brands, they are more likely to adopt brands that have a strong following among traditional suburban youth such as Adidas and New Balance. They are also likely to balance their urban music tastes with pop music artists like Coldplay or Maroon 5.

Another key nuance for the Sub-Urban cipher is within the technology and new media space. These consumers are heavy gamers and are predisposed toward consumer electronics, MP3s, and digital downloads. As technology becomes more advanced and capable of creating rich social experiences, badge items are more likely to be an iPhone, iPod, or new camera phone than a Nike sneaker.

Video game makers such as EA Sports also cashed in on the Sub-Urban cipher's interest in urban culture, especially the lifestyle of the Core Urban segment, with games such as Grand Theft Auto, which used the appeal of the urban automotive culture and featured popular Hip-Hop artists in authentic situations.

While Hip-Hop music and videos provided a window into the urban lifestyle, the videogame makers took further creative license to allow suburban kids to participate virtually in the lifestyle while infusing the brands most relevant to the urban audience in the process through product integration.

Sub-Urban Hip-Hopreneurs

As Hip-Hop and urban culture spread from the inner city to the suburbs, the list of successful Hip-Hopreneurs also broke the color barrier. Mark Ecko was a suburban kid who grew up listening to Hip-Hop music and painting graffiti. Mark parlayed his penchant for urban culture into a $300 million brand called Ecko, which became popular among suburban teens. Ecko also launched a magazine, *Complex*, which is a testament to those, like him, who are influenced by Core Urban culture but interpret it in a slightly different way based on their own, unique suburban experience and lifestyle such as skate-boarding.

Dave Mays has a similar story. Mays grew up in Boston and became a huge fan of Hip-Hop music, so much so, that he founded a small magazine while at Harvard University that he titled *The Source*. The magazine eventually became the "bible of Hip-Hop music and culture" and made Mays a millionaire in the process. *The Source* was forced to file for bankruptcy in the face of a string of industry controversies and financial mismanagement; it was eventually rescued from bankruptcy in 2008. True to the Hip-Hop form of reinvention, Mays went on to launch a separate publication, *Hip Hop Weekly*,

Contemporary Urban—Hip-Hop's Generation X

As much as I hate to admit it, while I am a product of Hip-Hop culture, I am no longer as cool as I once thought I was. I'm a parent, an entrepreneur, and my tastes have evolved and become more refined. As a result, I belong to the Contemporary Urban cipher. This cipher is comprised of African Americans and Hispanics aged 25 to 40. These are individuals who overcame obstacles or immigration on the path to the American Dream.

Members of the Contemporary Urban cipher are Hip-Hop's Generation X (30+) grown-up. While we still follow the culture, music, and fashion trends, we can't quite show-up at the PTA meeting wearing Timberland boots and a throwback jersey. Well, we could but that might be perceived as less than civilized.

HIP-HOP QUOTABLE

I don't wear (throwback) jerseys, I'm thirty plus
Give me a fresh pair of jeans and a button-up.
S Dots (Reebok sneaker) on my feet
Make my cipher complete."

JAY-Z, "WHAT MORE CAN I SAY"

I still may wear those Timberlands on the weekend, especially if I'm going back to hang out with some of my crew or want to channel my inner-thug. The important thing to note is Contemporary Urban consumers are really the architects of modern urban culture and a key segment that a lot of companies overlook because they're skewing toward the younger urban audience.

In fact, the Contemporary Urban consumer still wields tremendous influence in shaping the overall urban mindset. For example, the Contemporary Urban consumers' tastes in products have evolved and become more refined. As a result, a sizeable shift occurred within the urban apparel industry as brands moved toward cleaner lines and less logo-driven product to accommodate this move toward refinement.

I never thought I'd see the day when rappers would wear suits, but the 2004 *MTV Movie Awards* saw Kanye West, P. Diddy, and Jay-Z all in suits. On somewhat of an extreme level, **P. Diddy's manservant Fonzworth Bentley** personifies this phenomenon. As a product of southern culture, Fonzworth became relevant within popular culture with his self-proclaimed Gentlemen's Movement. Among other things, he appeared in com-

mercials for Burger King and became the official "arbiter of taste" for Hennessy before landing a reality series with MTV in 2008, *From G's to Gents.* That MTV series effectively captures, in name and intent, the evolution from Core Urban to Contemporary Urban.

It is important to underscore here that today's Contemporary Urban consumer is yesterday's Core Urban consumer. As mentioned earlier, when my friends and I were Core Urban kids growing up under the influence of Hip-Hop, brands became a badge for us to affirm status and project our aspirations. That mentality merely evolves as the Core Urban consumer progresses through life and gains additional exposure, resources, and responsibility. This explains why Contemporary Urban consumers are responsible for the growth of many luxury brands. They want products first and fast and are willing to pay a premium for them. As they come into more wealth, the options to decorate themselves and experience life's material treasures only grow. Without question, this audience is swimming upstream.

There is also an interesting gender effect at play here as many of the Contemporary Urban segment females have designs on landing the biggest fish. As a result, Contemporary Urban males who may have grown up in the 'hood but have now gained entry into a higher social class are able to "marry up" with women who are former Sub-Urban cipher members from a middle class socioeconomic background. Opposites truly attract in this case but the common denominator becomes the upwardly mobile lifestyle and shared urban mindset. These women are brand conscious shoppers with exquisite tastes. They are not shopping for brands based on a desire to project an image of status and "having arrived" but to maintain the image they have carefully crafted over time.

They also are the decision makers in the home and they buy luxury fashion brands to "upgrade" their men, as Jay-Z's wife, Beyoncé, sang in her hit song of the same title. Notwithstanding Beyoncé, these men have money and want to flaunt it on their women, which is central to the Hip-Hop mindset and urban male ego. Their women, in turn, open these guys up to high-end fashion brands. Ed Hardy, John Hardy, True Religion, and David Yurman benefit from this phenomenon, as do retailers like Neiman Marcus, Nordstrom, and Saks Fifth Avenue as well as high-end boutiques.

This is why you hear rappers now dropping brands like Manolo Blahnik, Jimmy Choo, Hermès (specifically the Birken Bag), Giuseppe Zanotti, YSL, Chanel, Cartier, Christian Louboutin, and Judith Lieber. They are vying for the affection of these high-class, Contemporary Urban women who have also become tangible symbols to reinforce the rappers' brand image and upwardly mobile lifestyle.

HIP-HOP QUOTABLE

I spent Four-Hundred Bucks on this,
Just to be like (expletive) you ain't up on this.

KANYE WEST, "ALL FALLS DOWN"

As the urban culture has become mainstream and the doors of opportunity have widened, the African Americans who are part of the Contemporary Urban cipher are in position to be the first to pass down significant wealth.

Individuals like Jay-Z and Usher now own stakes in major sports franchises and have offshore investments. They are living the life of opulence they once aspired to in their lyrics. Beyond the stars themselves, the critical masses within this contemporary urban segment have achieved success in corporate America and, increasingly, forged an entrepreneurial path in the pursuit of wealth.

At the same time, they are more financially literate than prior generations and have become savvy investors and key players on Wall Street. This segment could be a prime target for banks and financial services companies, which have yet to fully tap into this segment's potential beyond just high net worth athletes and entertainers.

These highly mobile moguls also look to marry style with technology, which has become necessary for their lifestyles. As did apparel and footwear, tech products became tools for self-expression, starting with pagers, "or beepers" in the late 1980s.

The primary market segments for pagers were doctors, contractors, and others in similar industries that required rapid response. It also signaled importance and status to the Hip-Hop generation which latched on to pagers as an outward symbol of an inward desire to project an image of being important or "living large and in charge" as we used to say. As an undergrad at Northwestern I self-activated my pager along with my good friend Marc Brooks so the ladies would assume we were just that.

In fact, Marc and I developed monikers, Mr. Large and Mr. Important. To this day, I will greet him as "Mr. Important" with a chuckle when I call or leave a voice mail message for him. Marc's story also personifies the Contemporary Urban segment. His father, Frank Brooks, is an African-American business icon and entrepreneur who founded the Brooks Food Group, one of the largest suppliers for McDonald's. Marc firmly grasped the baton from his father and is one of Chicago's leading entrepreneurs. Perhaps, ironically, Marc's first business enterprise after getting his MBA from Northwestern's Kellogg School of Business was a chain of successful wireless stores in partnership with

U.S. Cellular to penetrate the emerging urban market. Mr. Important indeed.

HIP-HOP QUOTABLE

A businessman with a beeper for a reason
Not like Tim
Because it's in this season

SALT-N-PEPA, "EXPRESS YOURSELF"

After making brands like pager company SkyTel household names in pop culture, videos, and lyrics, the Hip-Hop generation turned its attention to cell phones, which instantly became a fashion accessory and badge of status from their first arrival in the early 1990s. The original "brick phone" with the car kit was found in clubs, videos, and movies such as *New Jack City,* which starred Wesley Snipes as a notorious drug dealer in New York who exploited the crack epidemic.

Art was authentically imitating life in this instance as drug dealers were the early adopters and primary influencers for this technology within this segment because of their need for a similar rapid response, all during a time when brands, image, and self-expression were colliding.

For Contemporary Urban consumers, one brand, Motorola, best represents their tech migration. As the early leader, Motorola was the premium badge of the cell phone industry. Most came of age with Motorola and were captivated by the innovation of the Star-Tac phone that came on the scene in the mid-90s. Nearly all NBA players had one of these sleek, black phones in their possession. Aesthetically, this was a radical departure from the brick phone.

The adoption by the "rich and famous" became a signal downstream to the urban consumer masses that responded. The phone was also fairly expensive at the time, which made it exclusive and a must have for this segment.

On the heels of the Star-Tac, Motorola revolutionized another market with the Two-Way pager, which became a cult classic among Contemporary Urban consumers as it created a market for Motorola's two-way pager business. This product became so ubiquitous in the urban market and among the Hip-Hop generation that "Two-Way" became a brand name, eclipsing Motorola itself. The functionality was incredible as it allowed for instant, two-way communication and the maintenance of contacts that are crucial to this segment. The sleek design and flip screen gave the product style.

HIP-HOP QUOTABLE

Only way to roll, Jigga and two ladies
I'm too cold, Motorola Two-Way page me
      JAY-Z, "I JUST WANNA LOVE U (GIVE IT 2 ME)"

The brand was fairly oblivious to most of this when they brought me in for a discussion on reaching the urban target in 2003. Fortunately, Motorola had a savvy marketer in the ranks in David Rudd who was also a fellow Northwestern grad. In addition, my former Nike colleagues Geoffrey Frost and Stuart Redsun had joined Motorola. Geoffrey recognized the importance of engaging this audience.

Before his sudden passing, Geoffrey was largely responsible for reinvigorating Motorola and making the brand relevant through groundbreaking products such as the Razr. I dubbed the Two-Way pager the "urban laptop" for music moguls and other entrepreneurs in the Hip-Hop generation who spent less than two or three hours a day in their offices and conducted most of their business on the Two-Way. This niche within the urban market didn't need Microsoft Office in order to function effectively.

Motorola's inability to fully seize the Contemporary Urban market was to its detriment as it eventually lost the urban market share to Blackberry, which is now the clear leader among this segment.

There are nuances with the Contemporary Urban segment as well. Although I am still an avid listener of Hip-Hop and look forward to receiving a new artist tip from my rhyme partners Chris and Tony or fresh mixtape from close friend Gene who makes regular visits from his suburban enclave in upstate New York to his old neighborhood in Brooklyn to get the latest, my listening tastes have also evolved and my disposable income is spent on other things. As a member of the Contemporary Urban segment, I'm also less likely to attend a rap music concert, and most of today's Hip-Hop music is a far cry from the Hip-Hop of my generation.

As our research indicated, Contemporary Urban consumers are opting out of urban radio for Sirius and XM satellite where they can consume classic Hip-Hop, R&B, and Jazz. I pretty much exclusively listen to satellite radio in my car and will call up my friends to leave a voice mail so they can hear a song I'm listening to on Sirius Backspin with the legendary Kool DJ Red Alert. I can see them smiling when they check that voice mail and reminisce. Satellite radio has yet to fully capture this audience and stands to gain by proactively marketing to this segment based on such insights.

As the Contemporary Urban segment has matured, media vehicles are also opening up to reach this segment. Former *VIBE* Magazine publisher Len Burnett launched *Uptown Magazine* in 2008. *Uptown* is positioned against this Contemporary Urban segment and appeals to its tastes, aspirations, and upscale lifestyle. It's really the first magazine to flaunt the success and broad dimension of the urban market.

Also in 2008, another *VIBE* alum and Contemporary Urban entrepreneur, Kenard Gibbs, formed a media company called MadVision with two other savvy urban media executives, Peter Griffith and Anthony Maddox to acquire the rights to the Soul Train brand from the legendary Don Cornelius. This was a brilliant and bold move that makes them instant gatekeepers for multiple media platforms and content. MadVision is a play on Hip-Hop and urban vernacular that denotes an extreme talent or gift. In basketball, we would say Michael Jordan had "mad hops" (jumping ability). Or, a rapper had "mad skills." As the architects of modern urban lifestyle and pop culture, Contemporary Urban cipher members are really just warming up.

Vintage Urban—Global Innovators

While the Vintage Urban segment is a niche of Asian Americans, African Americans, and Caucasians aged 14 to 30, their influence as innovators extends beyond the United States and represents the global reach of Hip-Hop and urban culture.

At Nike, I was always excited about going to Asia. The response to the Jordan product was just amazing. If you have been there you know how much Asians adopt this urban culture and have created their own unique kind of existence around it.

Similar to suburban American kids, teens in Asia adopted much of the content and trends from Hip-Hop. They imported Western urban culture through television, Hip-Hop tours, and the NBA, and they developed an urban mindset. Because their exposure was limited, when they found pieces of the culture they could buy into, they did so wholesale. As discussed earlier, when Air Jordans were released, sneaker fanatics from Asia came to the U.S. to purchase the shoes in bulk and take them back to Asia to sell for triple the price.

While Nike frowned upon the practice, it alerted the product marketing types that the Retro product could be a business with a long life cycle. If you look at Nike's Jordan brand business now, the re-releasing of the retro Air Jordan shoes with updated colors and styles drives most of it.

Nike had a category called Limited Edition responsible for remixing and re-releasing the classics. It was an important category but was fairly small and under the radar until the company wisely applied resources and infrastructure to support it. With that support, it became one of the company's top performing categories led by the Air Force One franchise, which rivaled only the Air Jordan in popularity among urban consumers. The Air Force One was a 1980's low-cut basketball shoe that went for less than $100. Urban consumers gobbled them up whenever they were released. At a time when footwear technology has advanced tremendously and brands like Nike invest so much in technology and R&D, it is interesting that consumers want a plain, white sneaker such as the Air Force One with no "Air" technology, bells, or whistles. A small but important footnote here is the value of clean, white simple designs, an essential staple for urban consumers.

As with the Air Jordan, Nike introduced a limited number of pairs of these classic models to keep demand strong. Nike would eventually do Air Force One shoes for cities and music artists, such as Nelly, who penned an anthem about them. A secondary market was also created by teens, who designed their own versions of the Air Force One. Nike eventually brought some of them on as consultants. After the Air Force One, the Nike Dunk became a must-have for the Vintage Urban consumer.

With the success of Nike's retro business, other brands sought to cash in on the Vintage Urban consumer's thirst for classics. Brands like Converse and Pony were able to re-emerge and become relevant in popular culture and Hollywood. While the Vintage Urban consumer can be found in markets like San Francisco and the Northeast, the

global laboratory for this segment is taking place in Japan. Its chief scientist is **a Japanese designer named Nigo** who has embraced the retro craze and created a brand called A Bathing Ape, which became a popular but exclusive urban niche. Nigo grew up consuming nothing but Hip-Hop music.

He said he got to the point where he wanted to influence urban culture. His colorful sneakers, built off of Nike's classic Air Force One prototype, became a craze in New York. Nigo eventually opened a new store in the SoHo district. This is an extremely important shift in the paradigm as you now have an Asian influence on urban and popular culture by influencers who use their urban mindset to export culture and products to the U.S. from their consumer laboratory in Tokyo. In effect, the culture, which was influenced by Hip-Hop, is reverberating the influence and economic impact into the very market that spawned it, a fact not lost on Nigo.

"I've been listening to Hip-Hop since 1984," Nigo said in an interview to a Tokyo publication. "I guess I'm not interested in [developing business in] Asia anymore. Ten or 15 years ago, the previous generation was happy just purchasing goods from the U.S. or Europe. But my generation wants to be the creative center. We want to make what's new right here in Tokyo, and spread it to the world."

In 2004, Nigo partnered with Hip-Hop producer Pharell to design limited edition sunglasses for Louis Vuitton and tapped Grammy Award–winning artist Kanye West to create demand for the A Bathing Ape footwear and apparel brand.

As technology becomes more advanced and China continues to become a focal point and growth market for Fortune 500 companies, the role of the urban mindset will be critical in building bridges between Western brands and Asian consumers. Brands that realize this will surely maintain a first-mover advantage in the race for the loyalty of Asian consumers with an urban mindset.

Alternative Urban—The fusion of Hip-Hop, rock and skate

The Alternative Urban cipher represents the fusion of Hip-Hop culture, rock music, and skate culture. These consumers are aged 14 to 25 and are predominantly Caucasian with a growing African-American and Asian-American population. They are tech-savvy, action-sports enthusiasts, and gamers. They are also cultural transporters who are equally comfortable blending in either environment.

The relationship between Hip-Hop and rock, while seemingly at odds, is actually quite natural given shared characteristics such as ambivalence toward authority, making this particular cipher one of the most intriguing from a sociological perspective. It's also an extremely appealing cipher for brands because it totally transcends race and has a rich, historical context as these cultures clashed, then eventually mashed. Since the Alternative Urban cipher geography is also suburban, the mindset, preferences and lifestyle interests of this segment run parallel to the Sub-Urban cipher (similar to the way the Core Urban and Tertiary Urban segments do), albeit with some distinct nuances and attitudinal and behavioral differences. For example, unlike the Sub-Urban consumer, the Alternative Urban consumers are not going to rush out to buy the latest high-priced sneakers or apparel because 50 Cent is wearing them. They are more about simplicity, and prefer non-descript lifestyle brands such as Zoo York, but do also have an element to their personality that boasts material excess.

I previously mentioned super-producer Pharell Williams. Pharell and his partner Chad, also known as the Neptunes, embody this segment. Pharell, who is African American, and Chad, who is Asian American, are excellent examples of this cipher. Both have a rock sensibility and skateboarder's fashion style from their suburban experience but they have also been heavily influenced by a Hip-Hop culture of excess.

You'll see that fusion come across in Pharell. On the one hand, you may see him "iced out" with diamonds but he'll have on a brand like Von Dutch, which is popular with suburban teens. Reebok recognized the value of this cipher when it partnered with Pharell on the apparel line called Ice Cream. When making the announcement, Reebok Vice President Todd Krinsky said, "Reebok's licensing partnership with Pharell will enable us to reach a new cross section of consumers. Pharell's collections will fuse skate, hip-hop and alternative rock global youth cultures to reach a broader audience across all musical genres."

One of my favorite conferences is *Brandweek's* "What Teens Want." One year, I moderated a panel that included Johnny Schillereff, founder of Element, a company in California that produces skateboard equipment and apparel.

I asked Johnny how the suburban skateboarders like the Neptunes formed their urban mindset and he explained that the skaters had to go to the inner cities to skate because the degree of difficulty just wasn't enough in the suburbs. So they'd go to the 'hood and there'd be all kind of ramps and stuff that they could really get off on.

In the process, they were exposed to Hip-Hop music and culture. On the playgrounds and other places they'd get this whole vibe of Hip-Hop, the culture, and even some of the dress. Interestingly enough, modern skateboarders are a by-product of rebellious skiers in the 1970s and 1980s. They were on a parallel track with their urban counterparts who had discovered a form of rebellion called Hip-Hop. These rebels are now well into their forties but still plug in from time to time with the skate culture, just as Hip-Hop mogul Russell Simmons does for the Hip-Hop community.

I read Hip-Hop journalist Davey D's website and newsletter regularly. He is well respected in Hip-Hop circles and served up the following account in 2005 on this fusion of Hip-Hop and rock which is illustrative of the formation of the modern Alternative Urban Cipher.

The Connection Between Hip-Hop, New Wave and Punk
by Davey D

For those who wish to walk down memory lane, how could we forget when New Wave/Punk acts like Thomas Dolby, Tom Tom Club, The Clash, Blondie, The Thompson Twins, The Police, Depeche Mode, Human League, Tears for Fears and David Bowie, to name a few, were regularly heard within Hip-Hop circles especially in many of our "'hoods."

No offense to Run-DMC, who are often cited as the first Hip-Hop group to merge Rock and Rap, when we really go back and look at what was happening in the late 70s early 80s, we'll find that there was an often under reported important conversation and cultural exchange that was taking place with hardcore BBoys from the South Bronx and the disenfranchised rebellious New Wave Punk kids in downtown Manhattan on the Lower Eastside and in the Village.

It's important to note that this was not a natural occurrence that has often been erroneously stated, especially with the white kids coming up to the Bronx. It was a deliberate attempt on the parts of folks who had mutual respect and vision to build with one another. When you look back in time you'll find that both the early Hip-Hop and Punk/New Wave groups equally influenced each other. This admiration was reflected in Blondie's pivotal song "Rapture" where lead singer Debby Harry after being escorted up to a BBoy party at the PAL club where Grandmaster Flash was playing gave props to Fab 5 Freddy as well as Flash who blew her away.

As Davey D suggests, the fusion between rap and rock is not a new one. Hip-Hop mogul Russell Simmons and his Def Jam co-founder Rick Rubin first commercialized this fusion in the 1980s with Run-DMC and Aerosmith's cover of "Walk This Way." However, the history goes much deeper and a new chapter is being written as the boundaries between cultures are removed, music formats become less segregated, and these authentic cross-cultural exchanges reach the masses.

For example, Pharell announced he was forming a skateboarding team that will, undoubtedly, reflect the fusion between the Hip-Hop and rock lifestyles as will music from his group N.E.R.D, an alternative rock, funk and Hip-Hop group which continues to break new ground. Jay-Z's 2004 collaboration *Collision Course* with rap-rock group Linkin Park and producer Danger Mouse's *Grey Album*, which blended

samples from Jay-Z and The Beatles, also revealed the mash-up formula still worked. Other groups such as Black Eyed Peas (featuring Will.i.am and Fergie) and Gnarles Barkley have also spawned the growth of the Alternative Urban music genre and segment. **Gnarles Barkley** was a commercially successful collaboration between Hip-Hop artist **Cee-Lo and Danger Mouse** that spawned the hit, "Crazy."

Chicago rapper Lupe Fiasco burst onto the scene in 2005 with "Kick, Push," on his debut album *Food & Liquor*, which was his ode to skate culture and followed that up in 2008 on his second CD and lead single, "Superstar," featuring rock/folk singer Matthew Santos. Finally, Kanye West continues to explore new musical boundaries with a variety of rap-rock pop music collaborations including Chris Martin of Coldplay and Maroon 5's Adam Levine.

Such collaborations and fusion reveal both the essence and evolution of the Hip-Hop generation and the 7 Ciphers. Urban consumers take bits and pieces of the culture and weave it into their unique fabric to maintain a sense of self-identity while striving for constant reinvention. This sentiment is, perhaps, best captured by the acronym for Pharell's group N.E.R.D., which stands for No one Ever Really Dies.

Organic Urban—Keeping it real

Organic Urban consumers are similar to the Alternative Urban consumers in terms of simplicity, authenticity, and self-identity. They are primarily African Americans aged 25 to 49 with a significant white population. These consumers run parallel to the Contemporary Urban cipher in many ways.

They, too, were products of an inner-city background and Hip-Hop's Generation X but pursued their higher education at HBCUs, which heightened their sense of consciousness and primary socialization with other African Americans. They also stopped short of becoming absorbed with its material excess.

I like to call this the "anti-bling" segment because they're vocally opposed to the commercialization of the urban culture. For these individuals, it's all about being true to yourself. This segment is also defined as the "urban intelligentsia." They are well educated and socially and politically aware. As I mentioned earlier, cause-related marketing is an important vehicle to reach this segment.

Music artists like Jill Scott and India.Arie represent the mindset of this segment. Both are very organic and positive in terms of the content of their lyrics and music. This gave rise to the term Neo-Soul a few years ago. Neo-Soul attempts to capture the new generation of soul singers who are throwbacks to the golden era of soul.

As mentioned, they are products of Hip-Hop's Generation X so they grew up listening to classic Motown artists and soul music that is evident in their music preferences. Coca-Cola tapped into this segment when it launched its "Real" campaign a few years ago. The campaign featured artists like Angie Stone, Musiq Soulchild, and Common who delivered messages of positive self-expression. As stated, the members of this segment also include a significant population of whites who also came of age in the golden era of Hip-Hop and were influenced by the music and purest expression of the culture. Ironically, it is not unusual to attend a concert for artists like The Roots or Common and see a majority crowd of Caucasians like James O'Brien from Brooklyn, supporting real Hip-Hop music and representing the lifestyle to the fullest. Or, as Common put it in one of his lyrics, "when we perform, it's just coffee shop chicks and white dudes."

In addition to the racial transcendence in this segment, the Organic Urban cipher also speaks to the global influence of the

culture, especially as it relates to Europe and Canada. Musically, groups like Floetry and Les Nubians and even dating back to Soul II Soul represent positive images and music. During Hip-Hop's consciousness area, artists like **A Tribe Called Quest,** De La Soul, and Public Enemy influenced Canadian rapper K-OS (which stands for Knowledge of Self). Organic Urban consumers are also a fertile target for satellite radio because they are opposed to the commercialization of radio and want to be able to program music according to their tastes.

Implications for marketers and the 7 Ciphers

So what does this all mean? While most marketers understand the changing face of America, most have yet to find a forward-looking solution and strategic framework that works in concert with the core business, not outside of it. As a result, many brands still struggle with how to prioritize which multicultural group to focus on. At the end of the day, companies wind up falling short in an attempt to market one message to all of their customers.

The traditional, race-based paradigm is no longer effective, especially when marketing to the current generation. For them, it's really less about racial difference and more about identifying with others on the basis of shared lifestyle interests and mindset that cuts across cultural and racial lines. The 7 Ciphers serves as the framework to guide the process. While the benefits are substantial, there are three broad implications for using the segmentation.

1. **Target alignment and brand positioning.** If the wrong target audience is selected from the outset, the entire urban strategy and campaign will be flawed. The 7 Ciphers allows companies to pinpoint specific sub-segments within the urban market that have the greatest affinity for their brands so they can align strategy, positioning, media planning, product portfolio and marketing mix for maximum sales impact.

2. **Brand resonance.** By going beneath the monolithic "urban" perception with a visceral understanding of lifestyle and cultural nuances within specific segments, marketers can leverage the 7 Ciphers segmentation to ensure that their advertising and brand communications are written in the code of each cipher so they fully resonate with the target.

3. **Measurement.** As ROI has become increasingly important for brand managers and the path to consumer engagement becomes more fragmented and complex, segmentation approaches have become the rule, not the exception. The urban market has not had much traditional marketing discipline and measurement accountability associated with it, which makes the tool valuable as both a qualitative and quantitative instrument and overlay to existing tracking and brand health studies to track specific segments over time.

The net effect of this all is a new general market. A Pepsi Super Bowl commercial in 2005 featuring P. Diddy captured this phenomenon. The spot begins with P. Diddy needing a ride to an award show after his car breaks down. A Pepsi truck pulls up along the dirt road and the guy offers him a ride. P. Diddy pulls up to the red carpet event in the Pepsi truck. This new "trend" catches on and you eventually see the early adopters driving the truck with chrome rims and, eventually, it becomes mainstream as Carson Daly drives one. The following chart represents this effect of the 7 Ciphers life cycle and influence on the mainstream.

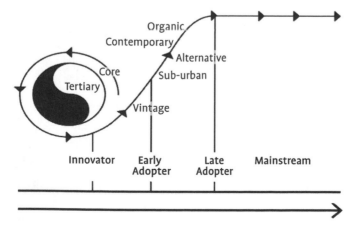

As mentioned earlier, there is an evolutionary pattern at play as individuals mature and evolve in their own consumer lifespan which overlap between the segments. Given the popularity of Hip-Hop and its innate ability to connect cultures and generations, the lines of distinction are often blurred.

For example, I can have a conversation with Alexis, my 14-year-old daughter, about Hip-Hop and cool brands and identify with her based on shared membership in the urban mindset, although my "Member Since" affiliation dates back well before she was born. This fosters a healthy dynamic between us. It also allows me to filter much of what she is adopting by providing her with the proper balance and moving her toward the highest expression of the culture.

It is my hope that the 7 Ciphers segmentation breaks down traditional barriers in marketing and fosters understanding of a generation that, throughout its evolution, has proven it has the Midas touch for brands from sneakers and cell phones to luxury goods and chrome 26-inch rims.

CHAPTER 5

Hip-Hop's

The question isn't what is Hip-Hop selling these days, it's what is Hip-Hop not selling. While most brands have come to the realization that the Hip-Hop generation can move product and create the brand halo effect, a select few have come to recognize the tangible sales impact the Hip-Hop generation can make by having a hand in the actual product creation process.

The Hip-Hop generation's influence has evolved from being a vehicle for demand creation through marketing, advertising, and promotions to playing an active role in product design and product development.

For the first time in the evolution of the Hip-Hop generation, we are witnessing the most recognizable brands across industries creating products born out of the urban consumer's distinct set of preferences and brand attributes which often run counter to their general market counterparts.

Who better to help brands enhance the form and function of a product than the very end users and urban content and culture software developers who have the "killer application" to breathe ingenuity into the utility of new products to fit their unique lifestyle needs and also give a seal of approval for the mass market?

Just a few years ago, the primary brand extension for Hip-Hop artists outside of the music industry was fashion. This was a natural place to begin as Hip-Hop music artists had historically been instrumental in making or breaking fashion brands from Calvin Klein and Polo Ralph Lauren to Cross Colours, FUBU, and Tommy Hilfiger. These brands became conduits of self-expression and aspiration and influenced the mass market through music videos and print advertising.

In the process, the artists were also able to see where many of the established apparel manufacturers and retailers were missing the boat with respect to fit, colors, and how to merchandise the all important "lifestyle hook-up" for urban consumers.

Some retailers, like Footaction, got it and merchandised lifestyle apparel brands with Nike sneakers, which is what the customer wanted. At Nike, my colleague Drew Greer headed up the limited edition (LE) category for Nike that housed the classic silhouettes, most notably the Air Force One franchise mentioned in the previous chapter.

The rap on urban fashion

While the other product teams, including the Jordan Brand, were working *internally* with our designers on color stories, Drew was looking *externally* at what the color stories were for the urban life-style brands. He knew the consumer would take his Air Force One sneaker and hook it up with those brands so he made sure the colors coordinated. He also knew that the colors the urban lifestyle brands were using were forward looking because those brands were inside the minds of the urban consumer. Product design and development were based on real-time insights, and the creative direction was coming directly from the source.

The Hip-Hop artists parlayed these insights and ability to affect apparel product design and sold rags for riches to Hip-Hop loving consumers around the world. They built successful brands by making product that the Hip-Hop generation wanted and marketed it to the urban culture as "insider brands" in the process. Tommy Hilfiger's brand decline can be traced largely to its failure to embrace the Hip-Hop generation, which had demonstrated true brand affinity for the product. Instead, it became urban legend that Hilfiger shunned the support of this target audience.

Whether or not this assertion is actually true, had Hilfiger broadened the brand access point and invited the Hip-Hop generation into the product design and development process, he might have found that their ideas on product styles, merchandising, and marketing could have kept the brand relevant. Instead, it slowly divorced itself from any positioning against urban consumers in favor of suburban kids who, in turn, were starting to gravitate toward brands such as Abercrombie & Fitch and Urban Outfitters leaving Hilfiger lost at sea.

Ironically, the urban apparel lifestyle brands have also witnessed their fortunes reversed recently. Their Midas touch lost some of its luster because they made a mistake similar to that of Hilfiger in the quest for mainstream validation. P. Diddy's Sean John brand is a prime example. In the late 1990s and early 2000s, Sean John epitomized the aspirational urban lifestyle and outright owned the "urban high fashion" position with price points that were just high enough to separate the men from the boys, literally.

For Contemporary Urban Gen Xers, Sean John was a welcome departure from the other logo-driven brands that they saw their younger cousins wearing, a fashion *faux pas*. Sean John had also become the brand of choice for millionaire athletes. It forced us to do our fair share of policing at Nike because many of our guys swapped the swoosh for Sean John while out in public because it fit their lifestyle to a tee (pun intended).

As Sean John charted its course and set sail for the mainstream, it drifted away from its core customer base. The Fifth Avenue store, print ads, and brand narrative no longer appealed to the Contemporary Urban target as Sean John attempted to move further upstream to swim with the bigger fish. This underscores one of the harsh lessons the Hip-Hop generation's fashion moguls learned as they moved from brand creator to brand ownership, particularly in the premium or luxury category.

It's important to stop here and reinforce the Hip-Hop generation's love affair with luxury goods. Throughout the journey from humble beginnings to redefining the American Dream, the Hip-Hop generation has looked to luxury and premium brands to affirm their status or project the image that they had arrived even if they hadn't. From clothes and cars to cell phones and drinks, the chase is always on for luxury goods and whatever comes off of the top shelf.

This aspirational quest for luxury by rappers even when circumstances proved otherwise eventually became self-fulfilling and the Hip-Hop generation figured out an unconventional path from the bottom to the top. The community celebrated them for this achievement and the brands they touched, chose, and started, became the gold standard in that celebration. These brands and products became the badges that gave them "all access" to the ghetto fabulous lifestyle that music mogul Andre Harrell so brilliantly coined. That is the essence.

While the Hip-Hopreneur's and moguls tastes had evolved, wealth had been accumulated and aspirations were realized, they also knew that there was a critical mass audience of peers who were also "moving on up" as part of this evolution, albeit not as quickly and certainly not televised. They naturally assumed these urban consumers would follow their brand upstream as it sought to compete with the established, high-end brands. Unfortunately, this proved to be an erroneous assumption. If these consumers were going to pay top dollar for a pair of jeans, it was going to be True Religion, not Sean John for the very reasons these same moguls would if they weren't pushing their own brand.

Lost in this equation were the masses of urban consumers who were the traditional fan base but did not have the means to afford the high price points and felt disconnected from the marketing and brand communications. In short, they no longer felt these insider brands were speaking for them. This same lesson holds true for Beyoncé and her House of Dereon line. On paper, the concept looked good. Whatever Beyoncé touched not only turned gold, it turned multi-platinum. In the process, she became a fashion icon and developed a phenomenal, top-shelf image. Surely, many of her fans would aspire to that.

Yes, but at a certain price point.

Beyoncé and her mother/stylist Tina Knowles parlayed their astute knowledge of fashion to create a line positioned at the top of the pyramid and befitting of Beyoncé who wouldn't want to compromise her brand image in a value or mass merchant channel. Beyoncé's licensing partners no doubt reinforced this premise through their pricing and distribution strategy. As a result, the majority of girls and young adults who do look up to Beyoncé, looked at the price points and couldn't gain entry. While more mature women also admire Beyoncé, their brand preferences lie with truly high-end, established fashion brands so House of Dereon was left in a grey area based on false assumptions and most likely in the absence of market research specific to the opportunity.

Beyoncé eventually, and smartly, segmented the brand with high-end distribution for House of Dereon in the likes of Neiman Marcus and creating a more accessible Dereon junior line for girls for the mass merchant department store channel at Macy's and urban specialty retailers such as Dr. Jays in New York.

This positioning and target audience disconnect was also a key learning for fashion and tennis icon Serena Williams who launched a high-end brand Aneres and faced a similar conundrum.

The temptation to do a "high-end" signature line is quite natural for celebrities representing the Hip-Hop generation but I have always felt they missed the greater opportunity to leverage their icon status and legitimate fashion instincts in partnership with an established fashion brand. It's the Tom Ford for Gucci model. For example, Beyoncé *for* Jimmy Choo would be a more authentic brand extension and aligned better against the target audience and distribution channel. Conversely, the mass-market audience has opened up significant opportunities for celebrities like Stephon Marbury (who opened up the flood gates in 2006 with discount retailer Steve & Barry's), Venus Williams, and LL Cool J to try their hand at private labels in the mass-merchant channel that gave them considerable creative license to impact product design and development.

Since the influx of fashion and apparel brands, the market has opened up considerably in recognition of the Hip-Hop generation's influence on product design and knowledge of brand utility in other categories. As such, companies are looking to those individuals of pure, Hip-Hop pedigree who best understand the lifestyle and its preferences to help them design their product in a way that resonates with the market.

Hip-Hop and the auto industry: Jay-Z Blue Anyone?

No industry has capitalized on Hip-Hop's Midas touch more than auto-makers. Recognizing the lucrative market created by the sports and entertainment elite and Contemporary Urban segment, the automotive industry has begun to manufacture cars to the exact, "tricked out" specifications of the urban consumer from 26-inch wheels to audio systems and custom interior design.

Media personality and car enthusiast, Funkmaster Flex, was the first among the Hip-Hop generation to land in the driver's seat for this trend with his limited edition Team Baurtwell Lincoln Navigator (complete with his own signature Lugz driving shoe) in 2003. Lincoln also did a limited edition Sean John vehicle that same year although it was priced out of the market at $85,000. In 2007, GM partnered with Jay-Z to capitalize on the unique brand position the GMC Yukon Denali had achieved in the urban market.

While the Cadillac Escalade was the perennial SUV brand of choice for the luxury segment within the urban market, the Denali was a more utilitarian choice, which offered better price value and presented a window of opportunity for the brand with the added touch of Hip-Hop impresario Jay-Z.

At the GM style event during the North American International Auto Show, Jay-Z escorted the **GMC Yukon Denali—painted a special shade of "Jay-Z Blue"**—down a runway during the exclusive, invi-

tation-only party next to GM's world headquarters. GM's executives were deliberate in touting Jay-Z's role in the product design process as part of the press announcement.

"Automotive design, entertainment and fashion have had a profound influence on each other and American culture for generations," said Ed Wellburn, vice president of GM Global Design. "Tonight, we're pairing a music icon, Jay-Z, with an automotive icon, the GMC

Yukon Denali. Our Global Color Studio worked with Jay-Z to develop a fresh, vibrant color that matched his goals and aesthetics. The paint uses a high degree of reflective materials that helps evolve the blue color spectrum."

Taking a page out of the Hip-Hop Marketing 101 textbook and chapter on demand creation, the Jay-Z Blue Denali was made available only in a limited edition run to stimulate demand among key urban influencers.

GM was certainly not alone in the desire to achieve a dominant market position in the urban market during this time. My friend Verdia Johnson brought me in to work with her advertising agency, Footsteps, on a similar recommendation for her Mercedes-Benz (MBUSA) client.

Specifically, Footsteps wanted me to work on the urban market plan to support the C-Class and GL, leveraging my 7 Ciphers segmentation and urban consumer insights.

At our initial meeting, the Mercedes executives revealed they had received an overture from 50 Cent that he wanted to partner with the brand. Everything he touched was turning to gold so there was some degree of interest. My agency partners at Footsteps and I agreed that this would be off-target, as did the brand manager. Ironically, we did suggest that the brand partner with Jay-Z on a limited edition C-Class which we felt would give urban consumers more reasons to believe in the entry level C-Class and continue to trade-up. This was also a more sizeable market, as the C-Class was a volume car, which is essential.

Similar to the discussion on high-end fashion brands versus mass-market brands, it is much easier to get the masses to buy into the aspirational notion these artists bring to products that they have a hand in. While not as elastic as their general market counterparts, price point is always an issue for the mass of urban consumers.

We eventually developed a program targeting the Contemporary Urban audience with insights grounded in the maturation of Hip-Hop's Generation X (ages 30+) who "came of age" with Mercedes-Benz as the aspirational, luxury brand of choice which validated their journey to success.

As opposed to a 50 Cent execution, which would have driven the brand off-target, we positioned Mercedes-Benz against the Contemporary Urban cipher and luxury market with the premise that Mercedes-Benz represents validation for those from humble beginnings as "having arrived." Footsteps' head creative Alvin Gay and his team eventually developed television creative for the campaign using the "Moving On Up" theme from the classic show *The Jeffersons.*

On the opposite end of the spectrum from Mercedes, Toyota's Scion brand moved its sales on up by establishing Hip-Hop as a key pillar for its brand positioning and built its brand platform on creativity, self-expression, and customization, all hallmarks of the Hip-Hop generation. It also created partnerships and sponsorships with underground Hip-Hop DJ's, concerts, and artist competitions. Scion's early success was based on its decision to give consumers an active role in designing their own vehicles.

Given my affinity for cars and understanding of the urban automotive culture, I like to play in the automotive sandbox. In Summer 2008, Ford introduced a revolutionary concept called the Flex. I was invited to the Dallas Auto Show as a key influencer, and had the opportunity to see the car first along with the media and attend an exclusive session with Ford executives as one of a few individuals who would help bring the product to market.

While not directly named after Funkmaster Flex, he would be designing a limited edition vehicle and had also played a role in some of the product's features. The DJ was also featured in the product video that was provided to dealers. In the video, he spoke about how he made certain suggestions to Ford on how to make sure the sound system had bottom, or heavy on the bass. When I test drove the vehicle for several weeks, I was blown away by the acoustics. With the volume barely audible, I could feel the bass, which was not too overwhelming but came through at just the right level. I eventually developed a grass roots campaign to support both the launch of the Flex and Lincoln MKS, which was a real game changer for Lincoln and was perfect for the Hip-Hop generation given its "modern luxury" positioning.

The resurgence of the Chrysler brand can also be attributed, literally, to Hip-Hop's Midas touch. The hot hand belonged to Ralph Giles, a graduate of Howard University and member of the Hip-Hop generation who ascended to the top of the ranks of the most talented car designers in the industry for his award-winning design of the breakthrough Chrysler 300 luxury sedan. Urban consumers instantly adopted it. The Chrysler 300 was bold and incorporated a classic silhouette and lines that were reminiscent of luxury cars like the Phantom Rolls Royce.

Giles was also responsible for the Dodge Ram and Dodge Charger, which rejuvenated the Dodge brand. The automotive industry has clearly realized that the best way to sell to the customer is to integrate the customer into the product design and development process.

Technology and Hip-Hop

Technology has not been far behind Detroit in the quest for Hip-Hop gold. In 2003, Motorola/Nextel forged a groundbreaking multi-year partnership with Russell and Kimora Lee Simmons' **Phat Farm/Baby Phat** brands to provide fashion and technology savvy consumers a wider range of mobile products and services to complement their style preferences.

The marriage between the Motorola and Phat brands included the development of co-branded products such as Motorola iDEN handsets, technology content, and accessories. "Mobile phones are intrinsic to the lifestyles of the hip-hop generation, and no brand does cell phones better than Motorola. The Baby Phat and Motorola relationship is exciting and will be bringing revolutionary items to market over the next couple of years," said Kimora Simmons, founder of Baby Phat.

The push-to-talk technology Nextel developed was very much a commercial solution, ideal for contractors. They observed that Core Urban teens had adopted the walkie-talkie approach to mobile phone use but weren't using them in the same functional sense.

As a result, Nextel created a sub-brand called Boost Mobile that used the same Nextel network but had a more youthful tone and pay-as-you-use option ideal for teens. Boost Mobile was successfully launched with a campaign featuring rap artists Kanye West, Ludacris, and West Coast newcomer The Game.

To Nextel's credit, it recognized that this kind of approach did not compromise its core business and its brand delivered a unique consumer experience and touch point. It was able to build the brand as well as leverage regional considerations, which is extremely critical when targeting the urban market. Boost Mobile recognized that in recent years there had been a growing pop culture influence coming from the southern region, particularly through music as outlined during the Tertiary Urban consumer profile. In the consumer electronics space, EA Sports also partnered with Simmons to break new ground with the Def Jam *Vendetta* video game that allowed gamers to choose their favorite "character" from the Def Jam Hip-Hop artist roster, including Scarface, DMX, Ludacris, and Method Man. The underground fight club video game put street-brawling skills to the test. "The only way we agreed to be a part of this was if EA could incorporate the Def Jam (read Hip-Hop) lifestyle into the game," said Def Jam president at the time, Kevin Liles. And they did, he added, from the cars to the distinctive soles of the fighter's Timberlands.

Hip-Hop generation and the spirits category

Outside of the automotive industry, the spirits industry has been the greatest beneficiary of the Hip-Hop generation's penchant for being brand creators from Snoop Dogg's "Gin and Juice" Grammy award winning song which helped revive the Seagram's brand to Busta Rhyme's club anthem "Pass The Courvoisier" which goes down in history as the most successful Hip-Hop product integration in any category. Urban consumers anointed Absolut the lifestyle drink of choice in the mid-to-late 1990s at clubs and happy hour events like First Friday's. First Friday's was a rotating social event on the First Friday of each month that was widely popular at the time among urban consumers.

For brands like Absolut, it is all about winning on-premise occasions such as this and encouraging trial and purchase. Unlike their general market counterparts, the behavior of urban influencers doesn't revolve around bar hopping. This is an example of one of those information gaps that cripples general market agencies from being able to engage urban consumers. They naturally assume a shared set of brand experiences and preferences based on *their* experience.

For urban consumers, drinking occasions are usually after work, weekend clubs, or lifestyle events, conferences, and destinations such as NBA All-Star Weekend. In this context, the drink one chooses sends an immediate signal and serves as another badge that validates status.

One question is always asked: "Yo, what you drinking?"

How you answer that question indicates your current status and how well you are in the know. During Hip-Hop's golden era, Absolut and cranberry juice was the refrain, particularly among the professional crowd. Moments such as this capture how the Hip-Hop generation's effect works and spreads virally. Marketers can take an insight such as this and turn the exchange into a commercial that rings authentically with the Hip-Hop generation. Heineken was able to do so with its infamous "Head Nod" commercial, which we'll discuss in the next chapter. It is one of those unfiltered cultural moments that could only have come from an urban insider who experienced it.

The case of Absolut

Absolut was very much positioned as a premium brand with the Hip-Hop generation with core brand values of creativity and self-expression which were spot on with urban consumers. When I arrived at Edelman in 2000, I inherited the Absolut account and was looking forward to leveraging these insights and applying my own touch to the brand.

My first task was to win over Carl Horton, a highly successful African-American executive who oversaw marketing and would later become President of the brand. Carl was instrumental in Absolut's early efforts to intersect the brand with fashion through the Absolut Africa event. Knowing what I knew about the contemporary urban lifestyle and the Absolut brand experience for this segment, I was concerned that the brand was not engaging urban consumers where they lived, worked, and played. Instead, Absolut was approaching the market in the traditional, cause-based "feel good" kind of way that never really moved product but was perceived as the right thing to do in case Jesse Jackson and Al Sharpton ever came calling.

I highly respected Carl because he was a pioneer in the industry. He earned his stripes in the 1970s and 1980s with my late father-in-law, Alfred Schexnayder who was a VP with Schieflin & Somerset. They were two high-ranking African Americans who succeeded in cracking the glass ceiling in the spirits industry.

While Absolut was taking the artistic high road and not engaged in the urban lifestyle trenches, it created an opening for other brands to erode its market share from the grass roots level with the assistance of an increasingly opulent Hip-Hop lifestyle and fueled by urban consumer innovators seeking to discover the next new thing in the spirits category.

First up was Belvedere, which Jay-Z and his partner Damon Dash made successful. This was followed by brands such as Ketel One and Grey Goose, which became the undisputed premium vodka brand of choice for urban tastemakers, primarily, at Absolut's expense.

I re-connected with Carl and the Absolut brand as part of the Axis agency multicultural team pitching its flavored vodka business in 2005. Absolut's research showed that the brand had lost favor and loyalty among African Americans. During the pitch, I suggested to Absolut that the declining brand loyalty was three-fold. First, the brand had not reciprocated the brand loyalty with any targeted outreach against the segment that connected to their lifestyle in an emotional fashion. Second, brown liquors such as Hennessy and Courvoisier had become the on-premise drinks of choice for the contemporary urban audience whose tastes had become refined. It was much cooler, more mature, and more aspirational to have a shot of Hennessy or Courvoisier.

Interestingly, as a by-product of product integration in Hip-Hop, this evolution and shift in urban consumer preferences from white to brown liquor could be mapped over the period between 1995 when

Snoop Dogg released Gin and Juice to 2005 when Busta Rhymes penned "Pass The Courvoisier."

Finally, while Absolut previously enjoyed badge status among African Americans, it was no longer cool to drink Absolut once it became so ubiquitous. This point is an extremely important attitudinal insight many brands overlook when targeting the urban market. The Hip-Hop generation, more than any other audience, is constantly driven by brand discovery. In other words, once everyone is doing it, it's time to move on.

With that in mind, instead of going after the flavored category, our recommendation was that Absolut evolve with the Contemporary Urban target's desire for exclusivity, discovery and premium brand association to make Contemporary Urbans the primary target for its new super-premium Level brand which was launching around the same time. In the process, these innovators would influence mainstream behavior while creating a halo effect over the entire Absolut brand to increase its relevance and grow the flavored category among African-American females and Hispanics. Hispanics were lagging behind the African-American market in awareness but indexing high with brand loyalty for the Absolut base brand.

While Absolut chose a different course, eventually partnering with Kanye West to support his concert tour in 2008, its competitor Diageo, the world's largest spirits company fully seized the Contemporary Urban market opportunity by stepping into the ring with the Hip-Hop generation's branding heavyweight P. Diddy hoping to take the premium vodka title away from Grey Goose with the Ciroc brand and "Art of Celebration" campaign.

While Budweiser made a similar gesture in naming Jay-Z as co-brand director of Budweiser Select in 2006, P. Diddy's appointment as brand manager for Ciroc was a watershed moment for the Hip-Hop generation and affirmed its impact on product beyond merely pitching it. During the announcement, Diddy demonstrated his own refinement, praising the manufacturing process of Ciroc, which is made from French grapes.

In his role, Diddy was given responsibility for the marketing, advertising, public relations, product placement, and events promoting the Ciroc brand with hands-on involvement in all aspects of the business according to Diageo.

"Sean Combs has a proven track record of developing high-end brands and we expect his alliance with Ciroc to follow suit," noted Debra Kelly-Ennis, chief marketing officer, Diageo North America. "We are confident that Sean and his team are the right partners to further enhance the luxury profile of Ciroc."

Some early indications, though, were that Diddy had forgotten the art of marketing to the urban market, which he had once mastered. As just discussed, urban consumers and the Hip-Hop generation don't like to be told something is cool. They like to discover it. Just ask the makers of Patrone. It's more about spreading buzz virally with this audience, initially, than dropping brand bombs. Granted, that viral discovery must be met with significant investment in order to sustain brand loyalty and first-mover advantage. With multi-million dollar budget in tow, though, Diddy made some of the same mistakes general market agencies make.

They toss money at the marketing mix hoping something sticks while their urban market counterparts take shoestring budgets and make them stretch through word of mouth and PR. That's why the best urban marketing agencies tend to be pretty efficient when it comes to ROI. They take smaller budgets and make the marketing dollars work harder. Instead, here was Diddy during the BET Awards after-party prancing about the stage like the teenager who had been given the keys to his parents' Porsche. The brand began saturating the media landscape with print ads and commercials, even running an ad during *Larry King Live* on CNN. How sexy is that?

Without question, Diddy has mastered the art of the celebration and will yield a significant impact on sales and brand awareness. The question Diageo will ultimately be faced with is, just how long will the party last.

A discussion on Hip-Hop and the spirits category wouldn't be complete without mentioning the fascinating case of Hpnotiq, a little-known premium vodka blended with cognac and natural tropical fruit juices. Hpnotiq caught on with urban consumers who were attracted to its blue color. In the spirits category, the importance of color, product design, and packaging, on winning over the Hip-Hop generation cannot be over emphasized. These factors alone are enough to encourage trial given the creative DNA of these consumers.

Putting that creativity to work, a bartender at P. Diddy's New York restaurant, Justin's, noticed many women but fewer men drinking Hpnotiq because they considered the fruity color to be too effeminate. The bartender, Victor Alvarez, mixed Hennessy with Hpnotiq to dilute the fruity flavor, resulting in a green beverage that became a hit and affectionately known as the "Incredible Hulk" or "Green-Eyed Monster." Welcome to the Hip-Hop generation's product development laboratory.

"Hpnotiq is very big among the hip hop crowd. Everyone is drinking the Incredible Hulk right now," said RED nightclub owner Jennifer Polsky at the time. "Not only is the cocktail popular with hip hop fans, but the artists as well. It has been referenced in song and has appeared in music videos. It was also mentioned in *The Boondocks* episode."

Wow. Let's see. How much was spent on R&D and marketing by Hpnotiq for that innovative new product? $0. What kind of revenues did the brand see from that one drink? Based on the anecdotal information provided by this nightclub owner, I think they made out pretty well on that deal.

Hopefully, during this chapter, you have detected a few patterns regarding Hip-Hop's influence. For starters, the 1990s golden era of Hip-Hop was the greatest period of innovation as the Hip-Hop generation came of age.

There were select brands that benefited most from this era and became ubiquitous in the urban market as conduits for self-expression and status: Nike. Motorola. Absolut. Mercedes-Benz.

Furthermore, these brands had several things in common with what I consider to be the core brand values and DNA of the Hip-Hop generation:

1. Creativity

2. Innovation

3. Self-expression

4. Ingenuity

5. Exclusivity

6. Respect

Brands who fail to remember #6, respect, do so at their own peril as the brand Cristal discovered. I consider Jay-Z to be the EF Hutton for Hip-Hop. When he speaks, people listen. He is an innovator and arbiter of cool who is trusted to know when something is or is no longer relevant. Jay-Z had an EF Hutton moment in the spirits category that I must underscore for those luxury brands that are inclined to think they can take the affinity of the Hip-Hop generation and its Midas touch for granted.

Cristal champagne was the definitive champagne for the Hip-Hop generation dating back to Jay-Z's Reasonable Doubt CD in the early 1990s. While P. Diddy has been associated heavily with the champagne, it was Jay-Z who broke it to the urban market. For more than 15 years it was the brand of choice.

So, one might think Cristal would let the good times roll. In an article published in The Economist's *Intelligent Life* Magazine in 2006, Frederic Rouzard, managing director of Roederer, the company that produces the high-priced bubbly indicated ambivalence about the cachet that Cristal had acquired among Jay-Z and his cohorts. Asked whether the Hip-Hop generation's fondness for the champagne might be hurting the Cristal brand, he stated, "That's a good question, but what can we do? We can't forbid people from buying it."

Maybe not, but as Cristal and many others have found out, you also can't forbid King Midas from removing himself as your primary brand touch point for the masses. In a cruel marketing twist of fate, Jay-Z used the same vehicle that propelled the Cristal brand into the consciousness of an entire Hip-Hop generation to immediately dislodge it: his music. I guess you could call it product disintegration.

HIP-HOP QUOTABLE

F*** Cristal, so they ask me what we drinking
I thought dude's remark was rude ok,
So I moved on to Dom Cuvee Rose
And it's much bigger issues in the world, I know
But I first had to take care of the world I know.

JAY-Z, "KINGDOM COME"

CHAPTER 6

The Intersection of

While the Hip-Hop generation was finally able to shift its influence into product creation, Madison Avenue needed no further convincing of its ability to foster demand creation. The intersection of Hip-Hop and Madison Avenue dates back as far as 1985 in Hip-Hop's formative years when the Fat Boys appeared in a commercial for Swatch watch. Before Rolex became a remote possibility, the Swatch watch was the must have timepiece for this generation.

When it came to TV commercials, as LL Cool J might say, Hip-Hop was jingling from the start. It was perceived to be the primary vehicle to reach the masses of African Americans, especially during Hip-Hop's golden era. From burgers and chicken to soft drinks and cars, Hip-Hop has pitched it all.

This mainstream visibility was also a double-edged sword for Hip-Hop artists who were constantly measured by how "real" they were. This blatant demonstration of commercialism would taint the images of already "hated on" commercial artists like MC Hammer who became a Madison Avenue favorite but clearly went overboard dancing in his trademark parachute pants for KFC's Popcorn Chicken in 1992.

Multicultural advertising agencies paved the way for the Hip-Hop generation to gain Madison Avenue acceptance, particularly African-

American agencies such as Uniworld, founded by Byron Lewis, and Burrell, founded by Tom Burrell. I will forever be indebted for the opportunities created by these trailblazers in addition to Don Coleman, founder of GlobalHue, Sam Chisolm, Eugene Morris, R.J. Dale, Carol Williams, Melvin Muse, and Vince Cullers, all of whom have agencies bearing their names.

These individuals broke the color barrier on Madison Avenue, although much work remains. In the process, they gave marketers from the Hip-Hop generation who are the "new jacks" as my friend Pepper Miller of the Hunter-Miller Group calls us, an entrepreneurial path to pursue on Madison Avenue that allowed us to set up our own shops as gatekeepers to the Hip-Hop generation and urban consumer constituency.

Most of these agencies have their legacies rooted in the post civil rights movement. As America was coming to grips with its changing racial complexity, it opened up opportunities for African-American entrepreneurs to start media companies and advertising agencies that would show the new face through media channels.

The government extended the civil right's mantra of equal opportunity to black media proliferation and helped make it possible for the legendary John Johnson's vision to depict the black family and experience through *Ebony Magazine* and Ed Lewis and Clarence Smith's *Essence Magazine* which gave African-American women a magazine alternative to depict their beautiful images, sacrifices, and struggles.

Hip-Hop's Truth In Advertising

As it relates to advertising and Hip-Hop, one brand, Coca-Cola's Sprite, can stake the claim as the true originator. Sprite was a major account for Burrell. One of the first advertising campaigns it did was with Kid 'n Play, a commercial-friendly group that still maintained relevance among hardcore Hip-Hoppers. Kid 'n Play was also distinctive, innovative, and creative so it was a good fit for Sprite which prided itself on the same.

The "Obey Your Thirst" campaign and creative platform was perfectly suited for the Hip-Hop generation's mindset of pushing the
boundaries of self-expression and defining oneself on your own terms
and not based on what everyone else is doing. On the surface, this
seems to conflict with the standard urban consumer notion that "one
person sneezes and everyone else catches a cold" and their desire to
fit in and gain acceptance and validation from peers.

While there is a strong desire to be part of the "in crowd," this is
never a wholesale proposition for the Hip-Hop generation and urban
consumers who must preserve individuality at all costs. The modern
urban vernacular interpretation of this is the term "Do You" which
became the title of Russell Simmons' *New York Times* bestseller. Do You
and Obey Your Thirst are one in the same.

Sprite recognized this insight and took it a step further in the mid-
1990s at the height of Hip-Hop's golden era. Sprite launched a full
Hip-Hop campaign featuring artists such as Pete Rock and CL Smooth,
Grand Puba, and Large Professor "freestyle rapping" in the studio. It
tapped into the self-expression DNA of the Hip-Hop generation. The
beauty of this campaign is that it gave the artists the creative space
to define the Sprite brand experience. These ads were as real as it
got. Some of the ads that were left on the edit floor were even more
authentic.

Interestingly enough, Sprite experienced similar growing pains
as the Hip-Hop generation itself did as it matured and found mass
acceptance. As a result, the brand struggled to find the cutting-edge
and reclaim the level of authenticity it enjoyed during this organic
phase. Brand managers and CMO's often ask about best practices in
advertising against the urban market and who is doing it effectively.
When it comes to Hip-Hop and advertising, I always cite Heineken. In
my opinion, Heineken took urban culture and lifestyle nuances and
drilled down deeper than any brand had gone before.

In 2003, Heineken partnered with Jay-Z on the heels of his ninth
album, the critically acclaimed double CD, *The Blueprint 2: The Gift &
The Curse.* In one of the Heineken spots called "The Takeover," which
cleverly borrowed its name from one of the tracks on the classic CD

and used another track from the just-released album as the music bed, Jay-Z is lounging at home with his girl who asks for a refill of champagne.

Jay-Z travels from room to room only to find each refrigerator loaded with bubbly. Clearly dismayed, he lands upon his mini-fridge, which is stacked with Heineken. At this point, oblivious to his girl's initial request, he returns to the sofa with only beer in hand and gives her a "What?" response when she expresses her visual discontent.

Heineken also chose the Grammy's—their "Super Bowl" moment— to introduce the 60-second spot and campaign to a prime time audience, which was a significant advancement for Hip-Hop and Madison Avenue. It was clearly history in the making for both the Heineken and Jay-Z brands.

"Getting an artist of the caliber of Jay-Z to participate in a Heineken commercial is a major achievement for the brand considering this is his first commercial," said Scott Hunter Smith, marketing manager at Heineken USA who undoubtedly leveraged his understanding of Hip-Hop to green light the campaign. "His ability to reach a diverse cross section of people with his music . . . fits with our commitment to find more and more 'occasions' for our consumers to connect with our brand."

Heineken followed up on the success of the Jay-Z campaign with a brilliant ad that capitalized on the growing popularity of southern Hip-Hop. It featured Hip-Hop mogul Jermaine Dupri and Lil' Jon, the self-proclaimed King of Crunk. In the spot, titled "Jet Bet," the two wager on who will win the most Grammy's. Lil' Jon is later shown on a private jet with a black bag, apparently holding the proceeds of the wager, while Dupri waits on the tarmac with his driver and Bentley. Lil' Jon exits the plane to personally deliver the reward. Instead of money, it is a 12-pack of Heineken. Demonstrating its understanding of the nexus between the Hip-Hop lifestyle and sports, Heineken broke the ads during the NBA Finals.

While the nuances in these ads were clearly effective, Heineken qualifies for best practice because the spots supported its overall brand positioning and tagline "It's All About The Beer." They didn't just tap into Hip-Hop culture and an artist for buzz, they peeled back the layers of the urban mindset and brand preferences to find the shared DNA between their brand and the lifestyle.

Heineken's most authentic demonstration of its understanding of the Hip-Hop generation through its advertising, though, was a spot called "Head Nod." The ad follows a guy as he moves through the nightclub making eye contact with various individuals and motioning with his head, seemingly in non-verbal agreement with their choice of Heineken. The strategic and creative brilliance of the ad is that it is deeply rooted in the authenticity of the urban consumer "lifestyle occasion."

I mentioned earlier the differences in occasions between the urban consumer and general market. This captured it. The club was exclusive. The crowd was sophisticated. The ladies were there. Furthermore, the brand took an iconic gesture and nuance from within the culture and put it in the context of brand choice and preference.

A discussion of the Hip-Hop generation and Madison Avenue wouldn't be complete without discussing Nike. While Nike and its agency Wieden & Kennedy have been careful not to overtly target Hip-Hop, they have been able to infuse some of their best commercials with nuances that reflect a visceral understanding of the culture.

In 1995, while I was working in the basketball category, Nike basketball produced a spot called "Revolution Will Not Be Televised," which was designed to introduce the newest faces in the game. Wieden & Kennedy used the song of the same title by Gil Scott Heron of the group The Last Poets. The Last Poets are considered by many as the true forefathers of Hip-Hop, and certainly modern day spoken word.

During the Civil Rights era of the 1960s, the group became a voice for the voiceless and expressed its discontent with the system and oppression through lyrics and simple percussion (or the drum), the essential elements of Hip-Hop.

Wieden bridged the generation gap between The Last Poets and the Hip-Hop generation by tapping conscious rapper KRS-One to do the voiceover. The spot was riveting to say the least and caused some controversy, which Nike never minded.

At the height of the streetball craze, a talented creative from Wieden named Jimmy Smith developed an ingenious spot entitled "Freestyle." The "bed" for the ad was simply the sound of sneakers squeaking on the floor while the ballers showcased their skills. It was Hip-Hop. Pure art.

The spot also introduced Luis "Trikz" Da Silva to the world. He became known as the best ball handler on earth, literally, traveling the world for Nike as a brand ambassador. The last spot Nike did, which will forever earn it props (respect) among the Hip-Hop set, is the "UMI Says" spot for the Jordan Brand. This spot featured another socially conscious rapper (and thespian), Mos Def, in an inspiring ad after Jordan's retirement which introduced our "Team Jordan" concept and players to the masses: Ray Allen, Michael Finley, Eddie Jones, Roy Jones, Jr., and Derek Jeter. Jordan eventually appears in the spot as he enters a grimy gymnasium much to the surprise of a group of young ballers and engages in a pick-up game.

I would subsequently tap Mos Def to perform at the Puck Building in New York for an Air Jordan release party I conceived in partnership with *VIBE* magazine, taking a page out of the music industry's marketing book. I even convinced my colleague, Air Jordan designer Tinker Hatfield, to make a rare appearance and observe the reaction to a frenzy for which he was largely responsible with the release of his latest incarnation. The crowd of urban influencers showed him "mad" respect.

HIP-HOP QUOTABLE

I ain't no perfect man
I'm trying to do the best that I can
With what it is I have.
My UMI said shine your light on the world,
Shine your light for the world to see.
MOS DEF, "UMI SAYS"

I loved working with Wieden & Kennedy because they were brand purists. In addition to Jimmy Smith, there were talented creatives like

Stacy Wall who did the Lil' Penny Hardaway ads, which featured come-dian Chris Rock as the voice, and were classic among the Hip-Hop generation. The beauty of Nike and Wieden's approach to Hip-Hop in advertising was that it was authentic in its execution.

In the case of the ads mentioned above, instead of finding a purely commercial rapper for a commercial, Wieden's creatives showed they did their homework by partnering with non-commercial, socially con-scious rappers, which supported their objective of creating thought-provoking advertising for Nike and gave it an organic feel. As a result, the approach was not overt but struck the right emotional chord by tapping into the right cultural nuances. This is the approach urban consumers prefer as I have routinely discovered when doing qualitative research on advertising concepts.

During focus groups I conducted and moderated for Coors Light, we probed pretty deeply into the issue of target-specific advertising. In other words, Coors Light wanted to know how important it was for African-American males to see themselves and their culture depicted in advertising. It was clear that they frowned upon brands that "were trying too hard," which always ran the risk of becoming border-line offensive.

Conversely, they also knew when brands were guilty of tokenism and placing the obligatory African American or Latino in the ad hop-ing it would cast a wider net and appeal to them. When discussing best practices, I tell clients that while done with the good intentions, the "one-size fits all" approach to creative execution will always fall flat.

Instead, for the respondents, the sweet spot was somewhere in the middle where they were depicted no differently than their general market counterparts but in situations that were authentic, similar to the Heineken examples mentioned above while incorporating the right lifestyle nuances. This fact alone made it a Herculean task for Coors Light to resonate with this audience based on its Rocky Mountain heritage and brand positioning.

One advertising concept I tested during the focus groups showed a group of brothers watching the game in a living room setting with the Rocky Mountains behind them. It just didn't work for them. They also felt that the Coors Light "Love Train" TV ads with the Silver Bullet train set to the O'Jays classic song did not speak to them, even though African Americans were depicted in the spots, albeit not prominently featured.

To its credit, Coors Light found early success leveraging Hip-Hop with television ads featuring super producer Dr. Dre along with a young Pharell and elder statesmen Quincy Jones in addition to a great spot featuring Doug E. Fresh in a backyard barbecue setting, both of which were very authentic.

Navigating the urban media landscape

While television was the traditional medium used to connect brands with Hip-Hop music and lifestyle, as the Hip-Hop generation came to dominate popular culture, more magazine titles followed including *The Source, VIBE, XXL, Honey,* and *Complex.*

These magazines gave brands a captive setting to embrace the urban market from the inside out and produce ads with a tonality, copy, and art direction that reflected the Hip-Hop lifestyle. This also created an avenue for Hip-Hopreneurs to build their brands, particularly fashion apparel, with the majority of their marketing spend going to print advertising in these publications.

In a similar fashion, urban radio came to represent another community-centric advertising platform for Madison Avenue. I have always liked radio as an advertising medium and included it in any media buy or recommendation my agency has handled. Urban radio affords a similar creative license as urban print and also creates a call-to-action and "surround sound" effect. One of the greatest benefits of urban radio is value-add. When done properly, a radio buy is more than just "spots" and can lead to promotional inventory, live remotes, events, sponsorships, online presence, and the all-important DJ chatter. This produces the "surround sound effect."

On Stephon Marbury's *Starbury* launch for our client, retailer Steve

& Barry's, the partnership we developed with urban radio conglomerate Radio One was a huge success and was instrumental in spreading the movement as the DJs gave attention to us on-air and reinforced the social commentary and narrative we desired. This wasn't forced or obligatory. I knew it would happen because, at its best, urban radio is also a community forum to discuss issues of importance to the urban community so the DJs willingly would talk it up for that reason alone. These DJs and morning show teams like *The Ricky Smiley Morning Show* on KKBT (97.9 The Beat) in Dallas, which is a Radio One station, are critical evangelists and opinion leaders in the urban community.

According to Radio One's 2008 study with Yankelovich Partners, 87 percent of African Americans listen to the radio in a given week. That lends itself to good reach and frequency as well as CPM efficiencies when you consider the plethora of value-added elements as well.

Urban radio has also become increasingly political, beginning with urban radio pioneer Tom Joyner and his *Morning Show* that featured regular, issues-oriented commentary from PBS journalist Tavis Smiley. The rise of ABC-syndicated program *The Michael Baisden Show* provides more evidence. During the 2008 Presidential Campaign, hosts such as Baisden and CNN-contributor Roland Martin who joined the *Tom Joyner Morning Show* became the liberal equivalent to Rush Limbaugh, Sean Hannity, and others from the right.

Madison Avenue recognized the power of nationally syndicated urban radio programming. In 2003, ABC Radio Networks signed a $200 million agreement with Tom Joyner's REACH Media to carry *The Tom Joyner Morning Show*, giving advertisers access to 8 million listeners each week in more than 100 markets as well as various multimedia platforms and sponsorships Joyner brought to the table. These included family-themed events, Black colleges, and the Internet. ABC Radio Networks forged a similar agreement with Michael Baisden in 2005.

As advertisers have increasingly turned their focus to the digital space, opportunities now abound for urban media players to expand their business models to position themselves as full-fledged urban media and content companies. These companies, such as Cathy Hughes' Radio One, serve as single source destinations to reach the urban audience both online and offline.

Under Cathy's and her son Alfred Liggins' leadership, Radio One has remained cutting-edge and taken a leadership position by investing in their interactive platforms. As Madison Avenue is being forced to apply more spending toward interactive and online media, Radio One is well positioned.

Closing the digital divide

In 2008, Radio One launched Interactive One and purchased several, leading African-American and multicultural sites supporting its goal to evolve beyond being just an urban radio station group to becoming a "media and digital content" company.

Just a few years ago, Madison Avenue was touting the so-called digital divide between the general market and multicultural markets.

Now, not only has the so-called digital divide been eradicated, but also use by multicultural groups has outpaced the general market. According to research from the Pew Internet & American Life Project, 55 percent of whites went online compared with just 38 percent of African Americans in 2000. In just four years, those figures changed from 66 percent of whites to 61 percent of African Americans.

According to an AOL study the following year, African Americans reported spending more time on the Internet (5 hours a day vs. 2.9 hours) than the general online population. Women are driving much of this usage in the African-American population. According to that same AOL study, 65 percent of African-American women "frequently or almost always" visit a product's web site when making purchase decisions, compared with 58 percent of white women.

As social networking takes center stage, Madison Avenue has surprisingly found Hispanics in the middle of the trend.

According to Jupiter Research, almost one-half of Hispanic online teens in the U.S. visit one or more social networking sites daily. I suspect acculturation is a key driver for this statistic as Hispanics seek online cultural experiences to stay connected with their peers and maintain cultural identification in the context of their acculturation.

Leveling the playing field on Madison Avenue

Bob Johnson and Black Entertainment Television (BET) have historically provided the only network platform for Madison Avenue to reach the urban market. Surprisingly, though, the network has faced a challenge convincing marketers of the value of the African-American audience. Viacom's purchase of the network and positive strides BET has made with respect to original programming and compelling upfront presentations has turned the tide somewhat but there is still much room for improvement. Media spending against multicultural markets still pales in comparison to the general market. The question is, who is the general market?

This disproportionate lack of investment in multicultural and urban advertising mediums has been exacerbated by a perceived lack of value placed on the African-American audience by African-American agencies.

Most of this can be attributed to a lack of understanding of the African-American audience as being monolithic and an assumption that they can be reached through mainstream channels. However, urban radio stations have encountered overt barriers to selling the urban audience based on "no urban" dictates.

No urban dictates became a significant issue for Madison Avenue as it was discovered that several companies instructed their media planners and buyers not to purchase airtime on urban radio stations. One such company was Quizno's.

These various dynamics present a combustible mix for Madison Avenue, which has faced increasing pressure for its long-standing lack of diversity and homogenous upper ranks. In 2007, the New York City Human Rights Commission began investigating the hiring practices on

Madison Avenue with 15 agencies agreeing to be monitored for three years on their minority hiring practices. The agencies reported meeting 24 of the 30 goals they set for themselves just one year later.

For instance, Arnold Worldwide, part of the Arnold Worldwide Partners unit of Havas, agreed that 30 percent of the managers and professionals to be hired in 2007 would be minorities, a goal they met. Some agencies, like Y&R, part of the Young & Rubicam Brands division of WPP, pledged that 18 percent of the managers and 30 percent of the professionals it hired in 2007 would be minorities. The figures they reported to the commission in April of 2008 were 27 percent and 46 percent, respectively.

"Going into this, we thought it was important to set high goals for Y&R and to support those goals with a clear set of initiatives," Hamish McLennan, chief executive at Y&R told Stuart Elliott of the *New York Times*. "We are going to raise the bar this year with the hiring goals for 2008 being set higher than last year."

While clearly motivated by the specter of the Commission and media spotlight and lawsuits, I believe diversity should be placed in the context of the business case for advertising agencies, not a human resource or legal issue. The more diverse a creative team is and the more reflective of the marketplace it becomes, the more effective and authentic the creative will be. It's that simple.

Furthermore, most agencies fail to realize that the Hip-Hop generation executives and creatives have creativity running through their DNA and are brand creators themselves. Most also cut their teeth working for general market agencies and are able to navigate both worlds effectively. While benchmarks and accountability are necessary at times, advertising agencies ignore such insights and talent at their own peril.

Regardless of hiring practices, Madison Avenue now knows the streets are listening and watching. Not only do the most popular and effective commercials feature urban themes and or talent, you can also catch them during your favorite prime time programming on the major broadcast networks and cable outlets.

Previously, most brands placed their ethnic or urban-focused ads on BET or during the limited, dedicated blocks of urban programming on networks such as Fox or UPN, who built a strong following with urban viewers.

In most cases, brands are now placing their urban-themed ads in rotation with their other mainstream ads or as their lead creative to drive awareness for the brand or a specific product during high-visibility programming, especially those featuring music artists. As I'll discuss in the final chapter, this paradigm shift does present a challenge for multicultural agencies, specifically African American, who now face the prospect of general market advertising agencies driving the creative and buying process for ads targeting urban consumers since the urban target is now within their range as well.

Make no mistake, though, the ultimate success of companies creating ads targeting urban consumers hinges on how well the agency reflects the nuances of the culture and lifestyle. This holds true for both general market and African-American agencies. African-American agencies are not exempt from passing the constant litmus test for authentic, urban "truth in advertising," especially considering the generation gap and disconnect between the old guard agency leadership and the modern realities of a Hip-Hop culture and urban mindset they no longer instinctively recognize.

Many of these agencies are top-heavy with management who represent the old guard and junior executives who understand these new realities but are virtually powerless and become mere tactical implementers.

There is a changing of the guard that these agencies will have to embrace that is akin to what occurred on the African-American political landscape in 2008 with the emergence of Barack Obama and its implications on the traditional civil rights leadership model for African Americans. Of course, the solution is an intergenerational one that triangulates heritage with new, innovative approaches by emerging leaders who have respect for the past but an even greater command of the opportunity at hand.

TOP 10 HIP-HOP GENERATION COMMERCIALS OF ALL TIME

1. Head Nod — Heineken
2. The Takeover — Heineken featuring Jay-Z
3. Real — Coca-Cola featuring The Roots, Musiq Soulchild and various artists
4. Freestyle — Nike featuring Luis "Trikz" Da Silva
5. UMI Says — Nike/Jordan Brand featuring Mos Def
6. All I Need — Coca-Cola featuring Method Man & Mary J. Blige
7. In The Lab — Sprite featuring Pete Rock & CL Smooth
8. Tour Bus — Coors Light featuring Dr. Dre, Pharell, and Quincy Jones
9. I Am What I Am — Reebok featuring 50 Cent
10. Pop Locking Girl — Mitsubishi

Hip-Hop goes Hollywood

Given the star power, commercial appeal, and stage presence Hip-Hop artists possess, it was inevitable they would blaze a trail from Madison Avenue to Vine, taking these boys (and girls) from the 'hood to Hollywood, and taking product placement to new heights in the process.

Leveraging their popularity in music, beginning in the early 1990s, Hollywood studios and network honchos would soon learn they could bank on Hip-Hop artists to pull in moviegoers and prime time audiences.

While Hip-Hop artists like Kurtis Blow, LL Cool J, Run DMC, Ice-T, and others made successful, cameo appearances in classic Hip-Hop films or movie soundtracks in the 1980s, it wasn't until the following decade that they took their acting game to the next level.

Furthermore, the production and compelling storylines around music videos increased significantly during this period of innovation and were now being directed by Hip-Hop Gen Xers like Hype Williams, who single-handedly transformed the genre by using music videos to tell stories. These videos were, essentially, short films and gave rappers the requisite "acting" chops their predecessors lacked. In fact, artists such as Jay-Z would acknowledge that they went into the studio and creative process for an upcoming CD as if they were writing a movie.

This growth in video production and techniques also afforded aspiring directors from the Hip-Hop generation with the opportunity to create storylines and develop film concepts that depicted the urban lifestyle and harsh inner-city experiences. As such, it was a natural progression for Hip-Hop to go from music videos to the big screen.

One director representing the Hip-Hop generation was John Singleton. He came of age under the influence of West Coast Hip-Hop groups like N.W.A. and the vivid portrayals they made of violence and the travails of young black males coming of age in Los Angeles, devoid of male role models and often turning to gangs for acceptance.

In 1991, Singleton released the Academy Award-nominated film *Boyz n the Hood*, about three, young black males (two of whom were brothers) growing up in South Central Los Angeles and their divergent paths. One was an aspiring college man, one an All-American football recruit, and the other a drug dealing gangster whose wayward lifestyle was responsible for the murder of his brother.

Undoubtedly, Singleton took the name of the movie from one of N.W.A.'s most popular tracks on its debut CD that further reinforced the film's connection and appeal among the Hip-Hop audience.

While the cultural significance of the film and its keen insight on racial inequality, absentee fatherhood, drugs, sex, and gang violence has been well-documented, the film was groundbreaking in other ways for the Hip-Hop generation. It marked the beginning of a rash of films that would transform Hip-Hop artists into bankable Hollywood stars.

In the case of *Boyz n the Hood*, rapper Ice Cube parlayed his critically acclaimed role as Doughboy in the film into a successful film career, spawning two film franchises in *Friday* and *Barbershop*.

Starting in 1991, a steady stream of titles hit theaters on the heels of *Boyz n the Hood*. These films included Hip-Hop generation classics *New Jack City*, about notorious Harlem drug lord Nino Brown played by Wesley Snipes, *Menace II Society*, *Poetic Justice*, *Sugar Hill*, *Set It Off*, and *Juice*, the 1992 classic featuring the late Tupac Shakur. *Juice* solidified Shakur's greatness as an actor for his stirring role as Bishop, a delinquent teen who spiraled into darkness after needlessly murdering a store owner following a botched robbery. The film also served as a coming out party for aspiring Hip-Hop actors and featured appearances by EPMD, Special Ed, Treach from Naughty By Nature, and Queen Latifah.

While this time period validated Hip-Hop's command of the box office stage, it also fueled critics who thought the films perpetuated stereotypes reminiscent of the blaxploitation era in the 1970s and questioned Hollywood's portrayal of black males and glorifying of violence through these films. Most of these critics accurately cited Hollywood's failure to show the full-range of stories within the urban experience. Hollywood's response? The only color that mattered was green so they gave the people what they wanted.

The growing influence of Hip-Hop actors also caused controversy with the establishment of African-American actors such as Samuel L. Jackson who lamented the fact that Hip-Hop artists were getting the best roles based on box office draw and not based on skills.

No filmmaker made a more indelible impact on Hollywood and the Hip-Hop generation than Spike Lee. Just as Hip-Hop groups such as Public Enemy and KRS-One challenged the lack of consciousness and balance of Hip-Hop's crass commercialism, Spike Lee's films brought balance to Hollywood's commercial "urbansploitation" of the 1990s. In the face of the flurry of urban dramas mentioned above, Spike built on the success of classics *School Daze* and *Do the Right Thing*, which is the standard bearer for Hollywood on race relations. Spike released *Mo' Better Blues* (1990), *Jungle Fever* (1991), *Malcolm X* (1992), *Crooklyn* (1994), *Clockers* (1995), *Get on the Bus* (1996), and *He Got Game* (1997). Each of these films provided powerful social commentary and appealed directly to the Organic Urban segment, or "urban intelligentsia."

Spike Lee also injected his social commentary into the advertising and marketing industry as well. In 1994, he released a satirical underground classic, *Drop Squad*, which put upwardly mobile African-American advertising and marketing executives on notice not to forget where we came from and to uphold the highest tenets of the culture when doing our jobs. In the film, the lead character is a token black employee at an advertising agency working on accounts including Mumblin' Jack Malt Liquor and the Gospel Pak, fast-food fried chicken with biblical overtones such as scripture-like quotations on napkins.

The "Drop Squad," a vigilante-style group of black deprogrammers, provided a hands-on cure for the token black guy by kidnapping him and exposing him to posters, slogans, and pictures of the family he had shunned during his meteoric rise in hopes of restoring his sense of community. While the satire was comical, unfortunately, it was art imitating life on Madison Avenue and self-image within the black community in many ways.

HIP-HOP QUOTABLE

As I walk the streets of Hollywood Boulevard
Thinkin how hard it was to those who starred
In the movies portrayin' the roles
Of butlers and maids slaves and hoes
Many intelligent Black men seemed to look uncivilized
And Black women in this profession
As for playin' a lawyer, out of the question
For what they play Aunt Jemima is the perfect term
Even if now she got a perm
So let's make our own movies like Spike Lee
Cause the roles being offered don't strike me
There's nothing that the Black man could use to earn
Burn Hollywood burn.

PUBLIC ENEMY FEATURING ICE CUBE AND BIG DADDY KANE, "BURN HOLLYWOOD BURN"

If image is everything, a clean-cut rapper from Philadelphia named Will Smith would do wonders to change perceptions of Hip-Hop artists in Hollywood. Smith broke down barriers and shattered expectations in true Hip-Hop fashion and became Hollywood's leading man in the process as the only actor in history to have eight consecutive films gross over $100 million at the box office.

Smith, born in 1968, is part of Hip-Hop's Generation X and Contemporary Urban cipher. After a successful Hip-Hop career, which officially bridged Hip-Hop with the MTV generation and earned him and his partner DJ Jazzy Jeff a Grammy in 1988, Smith made history in 1990 as the first Hip-Hop artist to star in a sitcom with *The Fresh Prince of Bel-Air.*

Smith went on to gain notoriety for his dramatic film debut in *Six Degrees of Separation* but saw his film career take full flight in 1995 with his role in the buddy cop film *Bad Boys* starring alongside comedian Martin Lawrence.

Lawrence was a fellow member of the Hip-Hop generation who had become a Hollywood heavyweight and pop culture contributor himself, coining terms such as "You Go Girl" during the successful run of *Martin* on the Fox network. Most people fail to credit the Hip-Hop generation with much of the success of the Fox network during its rise to prominence in the 1990s. In many ways, Fox was built off the generation's viewership and creative contributions.

In addition to *Martin,* much of the credit goes to Keenen Ivory Wayans for the sketch comedy series *In Living Color* that introduced the world to future entertainment titans Jim Carrey, Jamie Foxx, and a little-known dancer named Jennifer Lopez who was one of the "Fly Girls." *In Living Color* also featured live performances by a Hip-Hop artist each week.

Will Smith concluded his run on *The Fresh Prince* in 1996 in pursuit of his goal to become the "biggest movie star in the world." I think it's safe to say he did.

Smith's successful journey to become a "triple-threat" in music, television, and film is being followed closely by rapper turned actor, Common, who parlayed appearances in television commercials for

Gap and Lincoln-Mercury into breakout roles in *American Gangster* with Denzel Washington and *Street Kings* alongside Keanu Reaves. He also landed the role of Green Lantern in the live adaptation of the TV series *Justice League* in 2008.

Hip-Hop male artists like Will Smith and Common weren't the only Hollywood stars capable of being triple threats. Queen Latifah became a true entertainment triple threat in music, television, and film with television credits including Fox Network's *Living Single,* which was the most popular sitcom among urban audiences during its five year run, as well as starring roles in the films *Juice, Jungle Fever,* and *Set It Off.*

The New Jersey-born rapper also became the first in the Hip-Hop generation to do a talk show with *The Queen Latifah Show* in 1999. Latifah struck mainstream gold when she was cast in the Oscar-winning musical *Chicago,* which gave her an Academy Award nomination. She later returned to the big screen with the adaptation of the movie-turned-musical *Hairspray.*

This mainstream, commercial success also helped Latifah become the queen of Hip-Hop endorsements, raking in the dough, literally, as a spokesperson for Pizza Hut and landing the ultimate Madison Avenue prize as an endorser for Cover Girl cosmetics.

Breaking traditional marketing models

While brands like Cover Girl parked at the intersection of Hip-Hop, Madison and Vine, one of its competitors decided to build its brand home there, creating another watershed moment for Hip-Hop in 2008. Procter & Gamble formed a joint venture with Hip-Hop impresario Jermaine Dupri and Island Def Jam to form Tag Records, that will sign and release albums by new Hip-Hop acts. The label is named after P&G's popular brand of body spray.

"I've never seen someone wanting to devote this much money to breaking new artists," Dupri said during the announcement. "Nobody in the music industry has the marketing budget I have."

As the old music industry paradigm and distribution model continues to die, and the lines continue to blur among branded entertainment, product placement, and marketing, brands and companies are taking on the role of marketers. Procter & Gamble, Nike, Red Bull, Unilever, Converse, and Bacardi have all formed relationships with artists and provide compensation, promotions, and new distribution channels. It also winds up creating a better business model for the artist. The day will soon be upon us when the artists bypass the label altogether and go straight to retail where consumer product brands will be happy to underwrite the costs.

Wal-Mart, the largest music retailer in the country, has already begun to construct that model. After a successful release for the Eagles which sold 711,000 copies in the first week, they partnered with the classic 1980s group Journey with an exclusive release of a three-disc collection in 2008 which bypassed the record label middlemen altogether. In the process, the group retained most of the profits the record label would normally take in addition to ownership of the copyright and masters.

The marketing support also trumped the traditional label system. Irving Azoff, CEO of Frontline Management that manages both groups, agreed with Dupri's assessment. "With the downturn, the labels couldn't match the marketing commitments that Wal-Mart could make. It was well in excess of anything a label could do."

The record labels are not sitting on the sidelines watching. Several label executives with Madison Avenue experience are helping their label owners figure out how to adjust to playing in this new sandbox now that others are stealing their toys. Jeff Straughn is one such person. Jeff joined Island Def Jam from an advertising agency with the charge to carve out branding deals for the label's artists to raise their visibility. Capitalizing on the popularity of Def Jam artist Rihanna's popular single "Umbrella," Straughn and Rihanna's manager cooked up a partnership with the umbrella company Totes in addition to deals with JCPenney, Nokia, and Nike. I worked with Jeff on a similar partnership for one of the label's artists and Starbury.

Labels need more executives who think like Jeff and my friend

Camille Hackney, SVP of Brand Partnerships and Commercial Licensing for Atlantic Records, in order to have a fighting chance in this new battle for market share.

Just how far brands and Hip-Hop artists can push the envelope without compromising the very authenticity, which gave rise to its influence, remains to be seen but as the Hip-Hop generation has proven time and time again, and in the words of rapper Master P, there are no limits.

Jay-Z's business partner Steve Stoute expressed this sentiment to the *New York Times* in response to a similar question. "See that?" he asks, pointing to the picture in the center of the page, showing a General Motors SUV in a metallic blue concept color that Jay-Z helped design. "That's Jay-Z blue! We invented a color! There is no such thing as too far."

PART 3

HIP - HOP,
SPORTS, &
POPULAR CULTURE

CHAPTER 7

Inside

Making a $15 Sneaker Relevant

In Spring 2006, I received a call from a little-known retailer named Steve & Barry's University Sportswear from Port Washington, New York. They were looking to launch a $15 sneaker with an NBA athlete. Having graduated from the Nike school of performance and branding, I was more than skeptical at first. Hakeem Olajuwon made an unsuccessful initial foray into the affordable sneaker business model for Spalding years ago and, more recently, Shaquille O'Neal achieved a modest sales impact with his Dunkman line at Payless, but the line had no sizzle.

While Steve & Barry's was new to the signature sneaker business, they were no strangers when it came to retailing, so I was comfortable pursuing the opportunity.

For more than 20 years, the retailer had mastered the art of manufacturing supply chain to produce quality product at unbelievable price points. As students at the University of Pennsylvania, the founders of the company were convinced there was a way to make high quality goods for the collegiate market without it costing a fortune.

They set out to do just that. Upon finding some early success hitting the right price points, they were also able to negotiate favorable deals and leases with mall owners, often in second tier markets, and became anchor tenants commanding real estate and square footage. They built their business on a licensing model and soon were carrying t-shirts and other merchandise from nearly every NCAA school, eventually expanding into lifestyle licenses with GM and others.

Finally, they relied upon word-of-mouth and did no traditional marketing. If word-of-mouth is the best form of advertising, every day was a Super Bowl moment for Steve & Barry's as tens of thousands of shoppers frequented their stores on a weekly basis.

All of this eventually made Steve & Barry's the darling of retail and landed them in *BusinessWeek* with the distinction of being called the "fastest growing retailer you've never heard of." Now poised to inject celebrity private label brand into the mix to increase their cache, I realized these were very smart guys who were on to something. When I visited their headquarters that Spring, I was immediately struck by their culture, which was, essentially, an Ivy League feeder system. There were lots of eager to please but fairly green executives scurrying about. What P. Diddy's Bad Boy Records were to young kids coming out of HBCUs in the 1990s, Steve & Barry's was to young Ivy League graduates.

After an initial chemistry check, my first meeting was with President Andy Todd and senior management for our RFP response. Andy was extremely inquisitive and asked a lot of questions. I saw that as a good sign. Admittedly, he said, they didn't have much experience in the sneaker business but did what they did better than any other retailer. It became very clear they were a cost-driven culture. From the time the cotton was planted in the ground, they minimized costs every step of the way through the supply chain.

Andy was also a very genuine person who impressed me. We hit it off right away and my agency was ultimately awarded the business. Based on my history launching the Jordan Brand and coming off a successful brand repositioning assignment for Converse and launch of Dwyane Wade's sneaker, I knew there was no other agency better equipped to handle this task.

Steve & Barry's played it close to the vest and didn't reveal who the athlete was right away. In my mind, though, there were only a few athletes who could really pull something like this off with any degree of credibility and authenticity. Allen Iverson, Stephon Marbury, or Kevin Garnett. In my opinion, those three had been in the sneaker game long enough to guarantee sales and also had the streets on lock. Furthermore, while they each had reached the highest levels of the sport and were among the highest paid, they seemed to never forget where they came from.

Knowing what I know about endorsement contracts, I was pretty sure A.I. had a lifetime contract with Reebok and wasn't the correct answer. Kevin Garnett was new to the Adidas family at that point after leaving And 1 so that ruled out the big ticket. That left **Stephon Marbury.** Bingo.

Like most people who didn't know him on a personal level, I got a pretty good dose from the media about Marbury being an unselfish player who marched to the beat of his own drum. I would soon find out for myself as Andy and the Steve & Barry's team told me we would be heading out to his house to present the launch strategy.

One of the first things I told the guys at Steve & Barry's was they were not going to be able to scream the $15 price for an NBA athlete's shoe and get the attention of urban consumers. This was what they were inclined to do based on their usual approach of touting their "jaw-dropping prices." That would have the opposite effect as these consumers equated price to status and would immediately discard the brand before it reached the shelves, rendering even their budget-conscious parents helpless to force the buying decision on them.

Instead, I told them we would have to create a movement around this campaign to get consumers to opt-in to something greater than a pair of sneakers—a philosophy that was being espoused by Stephon Marbury, a product of Coney Island's housing projects who knew what it meant not to be able to afford high-priced sneakers. Instead of the usual "aspirational" formula deployed by sneaker brands of attaching an athlete to a sneaker and creating a TV commercial to seal the emotional deal, this model would be "inspirational."

It would also be supported by a social context regarding the high prices of sneakers and, particularly, the value being placed on those items by inner-city kids who often went to extreme measures to get them. I knew this sentiment had been bubbling for years, since I had come under fire for the issue while at Nike.

In addition, activists within the African-American community such as Jesse Jackson and Operation Push had taken Nike to task in the 1990s for not doing enough to support the African-American community. All of this boded well for the success of the launch from my perspective.

HIP-HOP QUOTABLE

I like Nike but wait a minute,
The neighborhood supports so put some money in it.
PUBLIC ENEMY, "SHUT'EM DOWN"

Andy talked frequently of their conversations with Stephon and their shared desire to "change the world" through this launch. They even wanted to incorporate "change the world" as a tagline. We thought that was a bit lofty as a claim and would leave all parties vulnerable since there was clearly a profit motive involved here as well. Also, I wanted this to be a first-person account from Stephon to consumers.

During this time, there was a popular phrase used in the urban market and within Hip-Hop culture when an individual wanted to affirm with you that you understood his point of view and where he was coming from in any given situation. After stating a position or point, he would say, "You Feel Me?" It was a rhetorical question in many ways meant to evoke a feeling of passion and at the same time engender support.

We ran with it.

We also wanted this to be about Stephon's vision based on his cumulative life experience. He believed you could still shine with a pair of $15 sneakers *and* feel good about yourself. It didn't have to be "or" anymore—pay $200 for a pair of sneakers or get laughed at. Sort of the lesson I learned in my earlier story about finding the money in the field and buying a pair of Adidas shell toe knock-offs.

Now, that same kid could go out and get a good quality, name-brand pair of sneakers at a reasonable price. In fact, my personal experience was a huge motivator for me to get involved with this campaign. Like Stephon, I was once one of those kids.

Thus, our tagline became: "This is my life, my vision. You feel me?"

My creative director Tony Lauher and I didn't stop there. We knew we needed to give a Hip-Hop feel to the brand. The beautiful thing about Hip-Hop Gen Xers is that we worked our way into corporate America but didn't have to leave the streets, and specifically, our Hip-Hop IQ, behind. Tony and I are kindred spirits in that sense. Besides being an extremely talented creative director who has worked in large agencies and run his own shop, we are able to "build" together on ideas that leveraged our Hip-Hop sensibility. We knew that Stephon and Starbury warranted such an approach.

To Steve & Barry's credit, they trusted Tony and me completely, a rare trait for clients in this business. Some within their marketing group, unfamiliar with urban vernacular, questioned if "You Feel Me?" as a tagline would offend some as sexual innuendo. We assured them that would not be the case. That trust would eventually become one of the greatest keys to our success, particularly as it related to creative, because it was so authentic and bypassed the usual corporate filter in a raw fashion just like Hip-Hop.

I knew that I wanted to ground the brand in Coney Island for the launch and create a strategic arc from Coney to the mass market. This is where Hip-Hop sensibilities come into play. One of my favorite Hip-Hop CDs of all time is Nas' Illmatic. On the cover of the CD is a childhood picture of Nas superimposed against the Queensbridge Projects where he is from.

Tony and I chose to replicate that idea for our teaser ad campaign concept. By doing so, we would allow consumers to understand that Stephon came from a place where he understood the struggles of everyday people and that was driving his vision.

We also decided it would be prophetic to co-opt certain classic Hip-Hop lines and put them in Stephon's voice in the copy, relating

to the philosophy and price-value proposition for the brand. For example, rap legends Eric B. and Rakim had a famous line "It ain't where you're from, it's where you're at." **On the copy, we put red ink through certain words as an editor would, changing it to "Where You're From Defines Where You're At." In this case, the editor was Stephon's inner voice.**

The beauty of this was it was actually something that Stephon would say as someone who proudly carried the Coney Island (and New York) mantle on his back, no doubt as a testament to his inner resolve, compassion, and basketball skills. It's important to note, we chose Hip-Hop lyrics from artists that represented our generation because they were now adults who came from the same experience, but had also achieved some success and were now parents of young children and a key segment for us.

I arrived at Stephon's house knowing he would be feeling this campaign. Without having met him personally, I knew this approach would appeal to his mindset. After brief introductions, the lead marketing guy for Steve & Barry's set the stage for the marketing discussion with an overview of the target audience and saying that the Starbury brand is going to appeal to everyone, "especially that Mom in Iowa . . ." Oops. The look on Stephon's face said it all.

"Who is this guy?" "I'm not feeling him," Stephon said.

Stephon is certainly not one to mince words and the media has perpetuated that perception of him as being brash and outspoken. However, as I began to know Stephon on a personal level, as many in his tight-knit family and circle know, I realized this perceived flaw by the media and public is actually his greatest strength. I knew that quality would also be invaluable to us as we began the PR campaign because his motivation for doing this was so very real and deeply personal for him. In part, that explained his reaction to the Iowa comment.

He went on to passionately say that he was doing this for the kids in the 'hood who couldn't afford high-priced sneakers. No MBA or classical marketing training required. He knew his target audience and promptly explained their insights and how to reach them. They wanted to still look good but not have to be held hostage at the store and pay $150. No more would they have to fork over top dollar and wear that same pair of Air Jordans for months and months until the soles fell off. They could now buy three or four pair at a time because they like to have fresh, white sneakers at all costs.

The marketing guy looked at me for a lifeline. He mentioned to Stephon that I had launched the Jordan Brand for Nike and would be handling marketing for the launch and was sure he would like the direction of our campaign.

That adjusted the thermometer some.

I explained to Stephon that we wanted to use Coney Island as the launch pad for this brand. His frown started to retreat some. I could still see his wheels turning in his head. "Is this the token black guy they brought in who's gonna come in here and try to manipulate my 'hood for selfish gain?"

Furthermore, I said, we wanted to tap into the Hip-Hop mindset of consumers to keep our messaging authentic and relevant.

Ok, getting warmer.

"Of course, you remember Nas' classic Illmatic," I said to Steph. Well, my creative director and I thought it would be cool to take a similar approach for the teaser ad campaign." I pulled out a mockup and put it on the table. He lit up. I explained that we wanted to shoot him in Coney Island as a next step. "No problem. I'm feeling dude, he said."

What most people don't realize about Stephon is that he is a man of the people. His people. Those who are without means but still have street dreams. The forgotten ones. He considers himself a voice for the voiceless. The perception that he is arrogant is often caused by the fact that he doesn't seek validation of a public with an insatiable appetite for celebrity, quick to love and quicker to scorn, because he has the respect of the people. If, as many have said, Stephon is either to be loved or hated, nowhere is that love and respect more obvious than Coney Island.

One might say well, of course they love him; he grew up there. Not so. I have been around countless athletes who leave their old neighborhoods never to return. And if they did, they would run the risk of leaving iceless, carless or faceless (as in reputation). I would quickly see this was not the case for Stephon. As one small but innovative example of his giving back to his old neighborhood, I later found out he would pay the barbers there to provide free haircuts.

We picked a picturesque day in Coney Island for our summer photo shoot for the initial launch campaign we would use in print ads and retail creative. I decided to tap my friend Jac Benson of Blacjac Entertainment Group to shoot a documentary around Stephon's Surfside Gardens housing projects that we would use for in-store video and distribute on the web to begin to illustrate the Starbury brand positioning and story.

I chose Jac for the project because I knew he would shoot the documentary with a Hip-Hop and urban sensibility but also the highest production grade as one of the entertainment industry's most sought-after producers.

We followed directions to what we thought was Surfside Gardens. Housing projects and basketball courts surrounded us. It was perfect. I called Stephon's brother Don to check on their timing. The story of Stephon's family and brothers has been well documented. They are good people and very close. Don was a superb baller and is a big dog Coney Island legend himself. He commands much respect.

My experience told me it would be important to connect with Don to make sure everything went smoothly. He said "Where you at yo?" I proceeded to tell him we were on a certain block. "That ain't our hood," he replied. "We can't do it there." It was a perfect backdrop for our photographers and videographers and the trailer was set-up with wardrobe, not to mention that was where we applied for our permit.

"This is Coney Island, right. Can't we just do it here," I said. I should have known better. I grew up in the Homewood-Brushton section of

Pittsburgh. No way would I do a photo shoot on Hilltop when I grew up on Frankstown Avenue.

"Steph's not going to do it there," he replied.

"Ok, let's pack it up," I told the crew.

Don met us and we followed him over to Surfside Gardens.

"This is where we're from dog," he said.

Moments later, a black Phantom Rolls-Royce pulls up. I asked Stephon during the meeting to bring one of his nice whips to the shoot and, perhaps, some of his jewelry to show that you can have it all and still not forget where you come from. The "and" not "or" seeds of the eventual Starbury price-value proposition I mentioned earlier.

He shunned it during the meeting but I was happy to see he did bring the car but was without any jewelry. I didn't know at the time but he was beginning to transcend spiritually so his "ice age" had come to an end. We were all leery of the public reaction but were quickly brought down to Stephon's earth as he got out of the vehicle. It was clear this was part of his regular routine, not just a photo shoot.

He yelled up to people hanging out of the project windows and gave pounds to onlookers (the demonstration of urban male solidarity a Fox News anchor quite ignorantly associated as a "terrorist fist jab" between Barack Obama and his wife Michelle during the Democratic primaries in 2008).

I was amazed throughout the shoot at how much he was revered in his old neighborhood. A woman who lived on his hallway came out to give him a hug and recalled stories of how he would bounce his ball up and down the hallway as a young kid, for which he promptly apologized to her again. He hugged all of the kids and it was also obvious they were used to seeing him around. Stephon's father, Don Sr., came by the shoot and recounted stories of his young sons growing up in Surfside Gardens and the values of hard work he instilled in them. Stephon would later tell me during an interview on the Coney Island boardwalk for the documentary how he and his brothers would run along the beach and sell sodas.

The only security Stephon needed that day was his right-hand man, Gaylord, or "G," as he is called. G is a class act, Mason and former police officer who was part security, part assistant, part advisor, and part mentor for Stephon.

G always maintained a professional appearance and demeanor. You'll see a lot of athletes and stars with "security" that are fresh from the nightclub the night before. Often times, their very image and presence provokes incidents. G was no nonsense and very firm but kept things cool.

We shot Stephon on the famous "Garden" playground where he honed his skills. The Garden is not just an ordinary playground. Legends were made on that court. It is quintessential New York street-ball. Cramped quarters, surrounded by chain-linked fences where the gladiators do battle sun up to sun down. The baskets had remnants of nets that swayed in the wind but gave no solace to a jump shooter needing a focal point.

We brought the varsity and junior varsity teams from Stephon's renowned alma mater Lincoln High School to the shoot as well to test the product and provide testimonials. To give the sneaker credence, part of our early strategy for the brand was to get **the "Starbury One" signature sneaker** Stephon would wear during the upcoming season on the amateur ballers and AAU teams during the summer before anyone knew the price.

I also tapped into my relationship with my friend Kenny Smith, former NBA star and host of TNT's *Inside The NBA*, to get Starbury plugged into his tournaments in Los Angeles and his camp at University of North Carolina.

Based on my Nike experience, I knew it was critical to have a presence at the grass roots level. Given the challenge of the perception and price point of the product we were sure to incur, it was even more critical for Starbury to win over this crowd and have them virally spread the word about the brand to give it a place within sneaker culture on merit.

We emerged with everything we needed to begin our teaser campaign. Stephon's sister Marcia helped us gather images of him as a young kid, which got our creative team excited. We eventually produced a full launch campaign set against the Coney Island backdrop and placed a media buy in key magazines for the basketball and urban consumer lifestyle target audience, including *Slam* Magazine, *DIME*, *XXL*, and *Complex* to coincide with the August launch of the brand and during the critical back-to-school season.

The initial teaser ads which hit during the late summer made no mention of price or Steve & Barry's as the retailer. They were all branded with the Starbury logo. While excluding price from the initial ads was a tough sell we eventually won. The retailer had no objections to leaving itself out of the initial concepts, as it was an unknown commodity to this target. It turned out that these two strategic decisions were among the best we made as part of the launch strategy because they allowed Starbury to grow organically.

While Steve & Barry's did not do much traditional advertising, we knew it was critical to have a presence in the print publications mentioned above. This was especially true given the authentic tonality and nuances of our ads and creative messaging, which we knew would fully resonate with the target.

I mentioned the benefit to an agency of working with a client who gives uninhibited creative license. Anyone who has done urban or multicultural advertising can appreciate this. Because there is such a chasm between the urban culture and corporate America brand managers, CMOs and agencies often are forced to water down otherwise potent creative elements they are absolutely convinced will resonate with the target simply because the client "doesn't get it."

In our case, Steve & Barry's "didn't get it," when it came to the urban market, but they were smart enough to understand we did. One such example was an ad we did based on a true brand insight and Hip-Hop nuance. From our perspective, Stephon was a modern day Robin Hood. Instead of taking from the rich and giving to the poor, though, he went out and found a way to partner with those with the resources to give back. One of my favorite songs by the classic Hip-Hop group Gang Starr is a song called "Robin Hood" where the group's lead

rapper Guru basically espouses the same philosophy Stephon was carrying out.

Tony was quite familiar with Gang Starr and
ran with it. **The eventual ad featured Stephon in
front of Surfside Gardens with the tagline "Want
To Know About My Robin Hood Theory?"** The
copy went on to espouse the price-value proposition of Starbury mixed with the social commentary we knew was essential to creating the
movement. We concluded the ad copy with, "well
those other companies, let's just say they like rob-
bin' the hood," a subtle but powerful reference to the lightening-rod
issue of high-priced sneakers.

As the August launch approached, I felt good about what we had
accomplished during the summer with the teaser ads, grass roots penetration, and website which began to feature some of the Coney Island
documentary footage Blacjac had produced. We were also starting to
see some chatter on the blogs of magazines like *Slam* from the ballers
who had heard or seen the product at camps or tournaments and were
giving rave reviews. Our plan was working.

As we got closer to the launch, there was concern over the limited
media reaction, which was a source of angst for the retailer because it
believed most of its marketing fortunes hinged on word of mouth and
the type of "free advertising" PR creates through media coverage.

During one of the media calls, the PR agency was going over its
pitch strategy and angles. It was focusing on Stephon's celebrity status
and how the Starbury product was "fashionably smart" with appeal
to budget-conscious moms. The only thing missing was the mention
of that mom being from Iowa. In other words, there was no social or
cause-context being planned to pitch to media about Starbury being a
movement that would eliminate pressure from kids and parents and no
linkage to Stephon's background, his vision, and how that correlated
with Steve & Barry's, a match made in heaven.

Steve & Barry's President Andy Todd was uneasy about this and knew Stephon would not be a willing participant in a full media blitz based on such a PR strategy.

Our smooth approach to launch just 60 days out would quickly turn to panic. One morning my cell phone rang very early. It was Andy. I knew something was up. Andy knew I was usually in the lab into the wee hours and didn't usually call until mid-morning. He told me that the entire launch strategy was now in jeopardy because the PR agency somehow allowed an Associated Press (AP) reporter to violate the embargo and release a story on the Starbury launch. The plan was to hold all stories until the official launch date. In PR, the embargo is a covenant between the media outlet and company. The media outlet receives all of the information, access, and photo assets, it needs to write the story but agrees not to release it until the date the company specifies.

Rule #1 in PR, of course, is not to panic and control the events. I learned this from the best crisis management experts while on the frontlines of the child-labor issues I referenced while at Nike. That was serious heat.

The inclination is for knee-jerk reaction because the media is calling and requesting comment or, in this case, upset that they honored the embargo and someone else didn't. Steve & Barry's executives and their lead PR guy wanted to go out with a release and make the full announcement. I thought this was a mistake and would only fan the flames further and told Andy not to feel pressured to react but respond on our terms. From my perspective, it was a soft launch far enough out from the real launch that we didn't compromise our concentrated marketing effort in August.

We did the obvious and asked the AP to take the story off the wire and pacified some of the media outlets by offering some exclusive access to Stephon and other Steve & Barry's executives. The story quickly died down. Andy subsequently asked me to put on my PR hat to handle it.

As we got closer to launch, I tapped into my Rolodex to make sure we rounded up the usual suspects. I called Oscar Dixon, NBA editor for

USA Today as well as Allison Samuels from *Newsweek*. I also contacted Bill Rhoden from the *New York Times* who was just finishing a book on the state of black athletes.

I first met Bill while I was at Nike and it was clear he shared a widely held view that black athletes were not doing enough to use their wealth and station to support youth and community. I knew Starbury would be right up his alley and made sure I built in a one-on-one interview opportunity with Stephon. In fact, my PR strategy was to conduct many media interviews like this back in Surfside Gardens so the media would experience the connection I initially observed and place this story in the right social context.

As I developed trust and a strong relationship with Stephon, I used my media relationships and worked a lot of these interviews directly with Stephon to put him in the best media situations possible and free of hidden agendas.

With just three weeks to launch, we hadn't secured any national TV or morning shows which Steve & Barry's thought was critical based on the suburban women's target audience they coveted. I was able to get to a producer for *Live with Regis & Kelly* through an associate and made the pitch knowing Regis is a huge New York sports fan, though sometimes critical of the Knicks. When I got the call they would take him, I was ecstatic.

This appearance also taught me a lot about Stephon. Of course, Steve & Barry's thought he should be in a "street" look because this would be the national debut for the brand and the product would be seen by the masses. Stephon told me he wanted to give a professional appearance. I agreed with him but didn't say a word to Andy. When we arrived at the ABC studios for the taping, it was clear that Andy and his partners were dissatisfied with Stephon's decision to wear a suit.

We were watching as Stephon was announced by Regis and Kelly for the segment and walked on the set. Regis greeted him with a firm handshake and began the interview with "Man, you look great. Like an investment banker."

The *Regis & Kelly* appearance was our national media tipping point. Interest picked up steadily from there. The website traffic was also exploding. Now, we were ready for launch. Steve & Barry's internal PR team decided to give an exclusive to *BusinessWeek* the Friday before and *The Wall Street Journal* to run the Monday of launch week.

I knew we still needed one of the morning shows to seal the deal. I had met Robin Roberts from ABC's *Good Morning America* at the U.S. Open a year ago through my attorney, Kevin Davis, and my friend Carlos Fleming of the sports management firm IMG. Carlos thought she might be interested in the story so I reached out to her.

I certainly used the *Regis & Kelly* piece as well as *The Wall Street Journal* article as fodder. Most importantly, as a former athlete herself, I hoped she would be moved by the altruism of an athlete who was much maligned but had the courage to use his celebrity to take a stand as the Robin Hood of a sneaker business which had grown out of control.

-----Original Message-----

From: Robin Roberts
Sent: Monday, August 14, 2006 12:36 PM
To: erin patton [mailto:epatton@themastermindgroup.com]
Subject: Wall St. Journal Story/Marbury

Hi Erin,

I think it's fantastic what Steph is doing. I saw his appearance on Regis & Kelly a couple of weeks ago...great job!

I'm not sure we can do something this week with Steph. I have been in contact with our producers trying to make something happen.

We will contact you if we can do that...thanks so much!

RR

-----Original Message-----

From: erin patton [mailto:epatton@themastermindgroup.com]
Sent: Monday, August 14, 2006 11:42 AM
To: Roberts, Robin
Subject: Wall St. Journal Story/Marbury

Robin,

Quick heads-up there is a story in today's WSJ on Steph's new line of affordable footwear and apparel and his mission to change the U.S. sneaker culture for kids and parents (Business Week story last Friday as well).

I'd still love to do something this week. GMA (and you) are his preference

---

We were close. After leaving the Steve & Barry's Manhattan Mall store in New York after a launch party and press conference walk through, my cell phone rang. It was Robin's producer who said they were interested in doing a story. It was on. I called Andy right away. Andy was a huge hoops fan so we often used basketball analogies. "I'm on fire baby. I'm making it rain from three!" I said. "You got GMA?" he replied, knowing that was my sole mission of the week. "You're on fire!"

PR was the Holy Grail for Andy so we had finally arrived. I called Stephon to tell him the good news.

"I'm gonna kill it son," he said. "It's over with!'

We filmed the segment in Coney Island with Robin Roberts and he did kill it. With each interview that passed, I realized that he had internalized his messages and was actually giving us and the PR team at Steve & Barry's talking points.

Unlike other athletes I had worked with or observed doing a launch, it was clear that this was not just a sneaker launch. This was a mission for him to change the world. Sitting off-camera during these interviews, I could see the direction of the interviews change to the direction Stephon wanted, even as reporters were forced to abandon their agendas in the face of his conviction and honesty.

He also began to reinforce key product messages we knew would be important to communicate to end users.

"If you take my shoe and cut it and half and take any other shoe and cut it in half, you'll see it's the same thing," he would say. It was a class move for him not to mention any other sneaker manufacturer by name. Even when reporters would try to feed him the bait and mention Nike or Air Jordan, he never took the bait.

The launch party took place on Wednesday, August 16, 2006, at the Manhattan Mall store and was very cool. Hip-Hop legend Biz Markie was the DJ and the event was a star-studded affair. To be honest, I didn't know what to expect heading into the press conference the next day. I knew some givens. Most New York press and Knicks beat writers had confirmed. We had a crew from ESPN's *Outside The Lines* working on a piece as well. I also brought Kenny Smith in to leverage his broadcast visibility and talent to serve as moderator for the press conference.

When we emerged from the green room and walked to the front of the store where the platform and backdrop was built, I saw a sea of cameras. The reaction was overwhelming. Media from as far as Germany had come for the announcement. Even the AP, who had violated the embargo, ran another story. Everyone was on message during the press conference and the photograph of Stephon, along with Andy and the founders Steve & Barry's holding the Starbury One sneaker, all smiling and donning business suits was the money shot that set the tone for Starbury as the business story for the rest of the year.

Our strategy after the national press outreach during launch week, which included popular syndicated urban radio "must" programs such as the *Steve Harvey Morning Show* and *Russ Parr Morning Show*, was to go full throttle on New York media for the next several weeks as the product hit the shelves. Stephon did appearances on every media outlet in New York. Big or small, it didn't matter.

He never said no unless it was clear the motives were not sincere which became increasingly rare as the media latched on to the story hook, line, and sinker. Stephon's willingness to make himself available was a key element of the PR success we achieved. You could almost hear the amazement in the voices of talk radio show producers and smaller media outlets typically shunned by superstar athletes that he was actually willing to conduct interviews with them and they wouldn't have to settle for a company PR spokesperson or a boiler plate quote from Stephon.

As in any campaign, there comes a time though when your advertising, PR tactics, media messaging and spin and grass roots activities yield to the voters who will ultimately decide your fate. It was time for the consumers to vote. What happened next will forever be etched in the annals of the history of the sneaker business. When we arrived at the Manhattan Mall store the day following the press conference, there was a line of people, which stretched from the main entrance, down three levels and out the mall onto 31ST street. Wow.

Christmas had fallen on August 17TH just in time for back-to-school. People couldn't believe that the shoes and clothes were only $14.98 in such a wide variety. There were four different **styles of sneakers**, jeans, hoodies, and basketball gear. Single mothers wept in the aisles in shock and disbelief.

Over the next several days, Stephon and I were brainstorming constantly. The Steve & Barry's internal team was also fully revved up. We didn't get any rest. We were all levitating. Then, the movement really started to take shape. We were driving around Midtown in Stephon's Phantom blasting Jay-Z's *Black Album* from his iPod with the song "The Life" on repeat.

"I don't why I get so high on, get so high, high off of life."

People stopped to stare at the source of the disturbance only to see it was Stephon rapping along to the lyrics in his zone. The news of Starbury was all over New York and by now the people responded with smiles and admiration. We were greeted as liberators.

One of my other favorite songs from Jay-Z's *Black Album* was also Stephon's. It's called "What More Can I Say."

There is one particular line in the song, which particularly resonated with me about Stephon at that moment riding through Manhattan as we both were firing away on our Blackberrys.

"A CEO's mind. That marketing plan was me," Jay-Z rhymes in the song.

Steph whipped out his cell almost on cue with that lyric.

"L Boogie, tell them to get a bunch of t-shirts and meet me on the corner of 31st and Broadway," Stephon said to Andy's assistant Lorena.

"G, head over to the store."

We pulled up in front of the Manhattan Mall store and Stephon got out. Pandemonium ensued. The t-shirts arrived. More pandemonium ensued.

"Give one to everybody," Stephon instructed one of the interns.

We walked into the Manhattan Mall and headed toward the escalators up to the Steve & Barry's store with a crowd in tow.

This was not a scheduled appearance. It was all impromptu. Customers couldn't believe it when he walked in. Usually, an athlete does the required appearances, media interviews, and retreats to his palace. Not Steph.

"How y'all doing. Thanks for supporting us," he said. "Brooklyn. What's good fam?" Stephon hugged mothers, high-fived kids, posed for pictures. He asked the ballers if the shoes felt right. It was then that I began calling him the "people's champ." We stayed for hours. As we walked out, I turned to see that the shelves were virtually empty. The manager said they were almost out of the entire inventory. It was only Day 2. The same was being reported around the country.

Back in the car, Stephon said it.

"We need to take the movement to all the people around the country to thank them for their support before I go to camp. Call Andy and set it up."

The Starbury Movement Tour was born—41 cities, 17 days in September. I went back to the lab to create the launch plan. I have a lot of friends in the music industry and, particularly, recall how successful many of the labels were at breaking new artists. Unlike the sports industry, they didn't just focus on the major markets. They built fan bases one market at a time, often in tertiary markets with an integrated approach of radio, local appearances and performances.

I wanted to do the same and keep it very grass roots.

We developed a plan blueprint around in-store signings at each

Steve & Barry's store in the local market supported by media out-reach and visits and call-ins to local radio stations courtesy of a media partnership I forged with Radio One. I knew the on-air talent at these urban stations would become evangelists for the Movement because it was a genuine campaign to benefit the urban community and their chatter would create additional buzz.

We also scheduled a public workout at the inner-city public high school that had won the previous year's championship or advanced to the state playoffs as Stephon prepared for the upcoming season in his new Starbury shoe. The student-athletes were also treated to a life skills discussion with Stephon.

The tour kicked off in Cincinnati, Ohio, but there was only a modest crowd on-hand, unlike what we had experienced in New York. Had we gotten drunk off our own Kool-Aid? I asked myself. "Where are we?" I asked an associate. "How far are we from Cincinnati?" It was clear we were quite a distance from the city. The first signing was good and had a decent turnout. We headed closer to the city for the second. It was Manhattan all over again. The store had multiple levels and the lines stretched outside the store and down several levels. Steve & Barry's stores were mostly located in rural areas, outlet malls, and other hard-to-reach places that made it difficult for people to access the product. Even though urban consumers had traveled considerable distances to the mall locations to meet Stephon and achieve savings, I would hear them asking him where else they could get the product and if they were planning to offer the product online or open any stores closer to urban areas.

The tour was a resounding success. We hit small towns from Marion, Indiana to Ashtabula, Ohio and met consumers who had never met a celebrity and were honored that Stephon would come to their town. Traditional thinking might shun visiting such markets for a marketing tour but Stephon knew these people would be customers for life. He also had an innate ability to connect with people from all races and walks of life and considered himself a "servant to the people." He never deviated from that.

We also visited larger markets such as Chicago and Detroit. Chicago was second home for me so I wanted to make sure we made a splash. I reached out to Jim Rose, sports anchor for ABC's Channel 7. During the workout at the local high school, Jim stormed through the doors with videographer in tow.

I had yet to see a reporter approach Stephon with such passion.

"I am a history major. This is history in the making," he said to Stephon. "There is Curt Flood, Muhammad Ali, and you. By reducing the factor of fear in these young people's lives."

While the signings became somewhat mundane, sitting next to Stephon allowed me to hear the rich stories of factory workers in Detroit who were recently laid off, families who were struggling to make ends meet and teachers who were grateful their students could focus less on what they were wearing and more on what they were learning.

This became real-time narrative for the brand and informed a lot of our marketing activity. Stephon would tap me when we heard one of these stories and I would pull the person aside, interview them and film their testimony.

The tour was full of such moments and we leveraged the content to the hilt. Steve & Barry's internal video production manager Abe Roofeh shared a Hip-Hop mindset. We used the content from the tour on the website and in-store monitors. Each city we went to received a reel in advance so shoppers could experience the tour even before we arrived.

One of my most memorable tour experiences was our stop in my hometown Pittsburgh. It was deeply personal for me given the obstacles I had overcome making it out of the Steel City and the problems that were plaguing the city with respect to youth and gang violence.

I was featured on the front page of the business section of both major papers and scheduled Stephon's public workout at my high school alma mater, Peabody High School. My mom also came out to the event and I was happy to tell her I finally found the answer to her question that dogged me since my days at Nike as we boarded the bus to head to the airport and our next stop.

"Answer to what," she said. "How to make the shoes cheaper," I replied with a smile.

While Pittsburgh was a rewarding experience for me on a personal level, our final stop in Syracuse, New York was the emotional climax for everyone. After 17 consecutive days of signings, media, and round-the-clock strategizing on the future of the brand, we were exhausted but still energized by the lives we had touched and experiences we now shared together.

Anyone who follows the Knicks knows they enjoy a strong following in upstate New York. We walked into the mall to a line that stretched for miles. As we approached the entrance to the store, the reporters were already assembled, smiling at the sight they were beholding. Stephon broke down and started crying on the spot.

Perhaps, in awe of seeing a layer peeled away from someone they didn't truly know, the media were speechless. A reporter from the local ABC affiliate stepped forward with a reassuring voice.

"How does it feel?" she said. Stephon broke down again before gaining his composure.

"To be part of something like this. To change people's lives is such a blessing," he said. "It's bigger than basketball."

The signing took hours. Stephon signed every single autograph even as we were warned we were compromising the departure time for our jet.

After the last autograph was signed, we all made a dash to the bus screaming wildly as if we had just one a championship.

In many ways I knew we did. We were champions for the people. The game was life and we were writing a new set of rules for the sneaker business. Between freestyle verses from Stephon, our excitement alone was enough to power the aircraft the short distance to Westchester Airport.

It would be just two years later in the summer of 2008 before Steve & Barry's problems came full surface and the retailer filed Chapter 11 bankruptcy in one of the most profound retail falls from grace on record. No matter what, the Starbury Movement will forever be etched in the annals of marketing history. Even if it didn't quite change the world as Stephon and his partners at Steve & Barry's originally envisioned, it certainly was a game changer.

CASE STUDY
How to Make a $15 Sneaker Relevant

1. Create a social movement

Our brand strategy was to make this sneaker launch a social movement that was inspirational. Most of the other brands were selling products and athletes for aspirational value. Based on the authenticity of Stephon's background and his persona combined with this revolutionary concept whose time had come, we knew we could market the brand on the basis of its inspirational value.

2. Keep it real

For creative messaging, we landed on the tagline, "This is my life, my vision. You Feel Me." This was authentic, urban vernacular that also supported the opt-in strategy causing the consumer to identify with Stephon's vision for Starbury. In addition, we co-opted famous Hip-Hop lines and treated them in copy as Stephon's voice.

For example, we took the classic line from Eric B. and Rakim that says, "It ain't where you're from, it's where you're at" and flipped it to say, "Where you're from defines where you're at."

This communicated to the consumer that we understood their mindset and that the Starbury brand was rooted in an authentic experience and Stephon's background, which was a huge motivation for his vision to make affordable sneakers and gear. Finally, we grounded the brand in Coney Island, shooting a documentary for the web from Stephon's old housing project. We also used images from the photo shoot in our prints ads, including my favorite which is an image of young Stephon, and superimposed them in front of Coney Island landmarks, similar to the rapper Nas' CD cover for his classic *Illmatic*.

3. Leave price out of the equation

We decided not to mention price in our early print advertising which defied Steve & Barry's typical approach. We wanted to give the younger urban consumer the opportunity to "opt-in" to the movement and shared philosophy of Stephon and Steve & Barry's and make the price value proposition secondary.

These consumers would have cooled to the brand at the outset if we led with price, which equates to status for them. Their purchase decisions are purely emotional, not rational and we needed to win over this audience even though parents, and specifically moms were the primary target. We knew we would be able to get the parents to make a rational decision once the product launched based on the price alone. Because the younger consumers saw the brand as relevant in a way that they could emotionally connect to, they would be willing to accept their mom's rational decision.

4. Build the brand organically and spread it virally

We penetrated the grass roots basketball scene strongly leading up to the launch to get the buy-in from the ballers that the shoe could perform. During the launch, we absolutely saturated New York media and conducted a massive PR campaign that created a nationwide ripple effect. I rode around with Stephon through the streets of Manhattan passing out t-shirts and greeting consumers.

Every other day Stephon would visit the store unannounced creating a viral, word-of-mouth buzz that produced long lines of people waiting hours before the store opened. Based on that reaction, we decided to take the Movement around the country to all Steve & Barry's stores to thank the people. Once on the tour, we hit all of the relevant touch points in each market (from high schools to radio call-ins to autograph signings). We really launched this brand the way record labels *used* to break artists. One fan at a time, one market at a time.

5. Know thy target audience

Having worked at Nike for so long, in particularly on the Jordan Brand, I knew we wouldn't win the "alpha" consumers and early adopters right away. I also knew the size of that market paled in comparison with the mass market of consumers for this price value proposition. We decided on moms and parents, tween ballers, and the 25+ crowd.

The moms were the sweet spot as they still controlled the purchase decision of the younger kids and we would make it a win-win purchase because the product was connected to Stephon who is an authentic and inspirational figure with street credibility to boot. Those moms have also been longing for an athlete to buck the trend and help eradicate some of the social ills connected to sneaker culture and cause kids to re-evaluate their values.

CHAPTER 8

Changing the Game

In the Fall of 1991, five young African-American men arrived at the University of Michigan as the greatest recruiting class in the history of college basketball. And they brought Hip-Hop with them. They were

even given a moniker like most Hip-Hop groups. The "Fab Five" achieved monumental success on the court and would also define an era that would leave the Hip-Hop generation's unmistakable imprint on sports. It is important to note here that the Fab Five were following in the Nike Dunk footsteps of the Georgetown Hoyas, led by Patrick Ewing. The Hoyas were the first team from an elite university to bring Hip-Hop flair from the 'hood to the NCAA hardwood. They had their own sneakers, a Black coach, all Black players and represented the East Coast, all of which added up to lots of brand affinity from the Hip-Hop generation. I am not sure if the licensing folks at Georgetown knew it, but the urban market played a huge role in sales of Georgetown Hoyas product during that period.

Just as their peers did through music, the Fab Five changed the game of basketball itself with creativity, self-expression, and by exuding the undeniable trait of Hip-Hop and urban culture. Swagger. Swagger is a confidence and attitude that is manifest through personal style and demeanor. From their all-black socks and baggy shorts to fresh Nike sneakers, Chris Webber, Juwan Howard, Jalen Rose, Jimmy King, and Ray Jackson were Hip-Hop. They were basketball's equivalent to the Wu-Tang Clan. Every member of the group possessed raw, individual talent and was capable of breaking out solo on the opposition at any moment, but thrived best in the group dynamic.

Without question, Hip-Hop culture and sports have become even more inextricably linked since the Fab Five changed the game. That impact is most evident in basketball. Clearly, most of this can be attributed to the fact that the majority of present-day basketball players come from the same inner-city environments as Hip-Hop artists. They came of age during Hip-Hop's golden era in the early 1990s. Much of this played out in New York and the East Coast where Hip-Hop originated.

The only difference is that one picked up a basketball while the other picked up the microphone. In some cases, both. Allen Iverson, Kobe, and Shaq have all released Hip-Hop records with Shaq coming the closest to being able to actually claim the dual status of MC and MVP. "The diesel" does have skills. It has been well documented that Hip-Hop artists want to be NBA ballers and NBA ballers want to be Hip-Hop artists. LeBron James places his hands together after a dunk in the form of the Roc-A-Fella dynasty sign while Jay-Z sits courtside.

While much of this has to do with an identification based on traveling the same journey from rags to riches and now sharing the same tax bracket, much of it has to do with the urban culture insight and vernacular we used for one of the Starbury advertising campaigns: "Game Recognize Game." The NBA athletes marvel at the skills of Hip-Hop artists and relate to the realism of the music that helps put them in the proper mindset before competition. Those Bose headphones the players wear from the bus to the arena are not just for show. They want to feel the music before they do battle.

Meanwhile, the Hip-Hop artists look at the NBA athletes as representing the same qualities they bring to the stage. Creativity. Style. Aggression. Energy. Self-expression. Furthermore, NBA basket-

ball simply moves at the same frenetic pace of Hip-Hop. This is why
the And 1 Mixtape achieved cult-like status in the urban market and
was so effective.

The And 1 Mixtape took Hip-Hop
music and edited it against a highlight
reel of basketball action. It was like
peanut butter and chocolate coming
together to form a Reese's cup. It just
works together. And 1 took it a step
further and actually used under-
ground Hip-Hop tracks whose lyrics even reinforced some of the
action. In short, ballers and Hip-Hop artists both have the same swagger that only comes from the streets. Certainly, you will find NFL players and some MLB players who have a true appreciation for Hip-Hop
and bring a Hip-Hop mindset and flair to their respective sports, but the
socialization of the athletes into the sport is what makes the difference.
For inner-city kids, hoop dreams and street dreams are one.

Basketball is played in the inner city. No equipment is necessary. All
you need to play is a ball, skills, some desire, and even more attitude.
For an aspiring rapper in the same environment, all you need is a pen,
a pad, rhyming skills, some desire and attitude.

Furthermore, both are attracted to and driven by the allure of
attaining overnight celebrity status and riches. Basketball players are
overnight success stories that go straight from the playground and
high school to the NBA and national spotlight (with one year of college at the most).

Kevin Garnett was a legend coming out of Farragut High School
in Chicago to become the first-round draft pick of the Minnesota Tim-
berwolves. He went from Kevin Garnett with ridiculous skills to KG,
the NBA's highest-paid player. Overnight.

This blueprint is similar to the allure and path to success for young
males with dreams of becoming a Hip-Hop artist. One year, he is Chris-
topher Wallace from the neighborhood who has skills to rhyme and,
just like that, he becomes Notorious B.I.G. signed to P. Diddy's Bad Boy
Records. Rags to riches overnight.

We used to fuss when the landlord dissed us
No heat. Wonder why Christmas missed us.
Birthdays was the worst days
Now we sip champagne when we thirstay."

NOTORIOUS B.I.G., "JUICY"

Changing times at the NBA

These external cultural and social trends that shape and drive both participation and spectators toward the game of basketball created a conundrum for the NBA in the post-Michael Jordan era. At the dawn of the new millennium they grappled with balancing a sports product that was becoming increasingly Hip-Hop with a core target audience that was mainstream and becoming increasingly corporate.

At the same time, the NBA did not want to disenfranchise the younger generation of fans, specifically white suburban kids, who were also coming of age with an urban mindset. The kids thought **Allen Iverson** was the heir to the NBA's marketing throne vacated by Jordan instead of the more polished Grant Hill the league favored.

Perhaps unfairly, Iverson became the poster child for the NBA's cultural identity crisis. "Bubbachuck," as he was affectionately known in the Hampton Roads area in Virginia where he grew up, was a phenomenal athlete in basketball and football. He led his Bethel High School team to the state championship as a high school junior.

On Valentine's Day of 1993, Iverson and a group of his friends encountered a racial incident and subsequent altercation with a group of white teenagers at a bowling alley and a huge fight erupted. Iverson and his friends were the only people arrested. Iverson was convicted as an adult on the felony charge of maiming by mob, a rarely used Virginia statute that was, ironically, designed to combat lynching. Iverson spent four months at a correctional facility in Virginia before

Virginia Governor Douglas Wilder, the state's first black governor, granted him clemency. The incident threatened his future and clearly scarred him as he felt he was treated unfairly by the judicial system. The Virginia Court of Appeals eventually overturned his conviction due to lack of evidence.

He later attended Georgetown University and benefited tremendously from his tutelage under legendary Coach John Thompson who no doubt understood the trajectory of Iverson's background and potential culture clash at a predominantly white university and provided safe haven along with establishing firm boundaries as the father figure Iverson lacked.

"Coach was like a father figure to me. . . . Ninety percent of having a relationship with him is things that occur off the court," Iverson said at the time.

Once in the league, though, Iverson found himself trying to be accepted for who he was at a time when the NBA was searching for someone who could accept who the league wanted him to be. And Jordan he was not. Iverson's image of braids and tattoos ran counter to Jordan's tailored suits and refinement. The more the league juxtaposed the two and forced the issue, the more Iverson seemed determined to outwardly rebel.

This attitude is central to the core Hip-Hop mindset where being true to oneself and bucking authority figures is paramount. For NBA players, this is often exacerbated by an inner-circle of friends and family who provide a familiar, safe haven and reinforce the feeling of rebellion in the face of a "system" that appears to oppress the natural inclination for freedom of expression. As a result, it fosters a "Me Against The World" mentality as the late rapper Tupac Shakur professed in his classic song on the CD of the same title. It's also akin to teenagers turning the music up louder when parents ask them to turn the "garbage" music down, or why young urban males let their pants sag lower when the teachers and authority figures at school criticize them for it.

As the NBA would soon learn, it is difficult to expect young inner-city black males to conform to a set of rules in a system dictated by white males, especially when the black males come from an environment where that same authority system is perceived, correctly or incorrectly, as constructing rules against them. And, especially when these young, inner-city black males are now filthy rich. Couple that with a lack of exposure and frame of reference for these athletes to see beyond their environment and the result is a clash of cultures and egos that becomes a self-fulfilling prophecy for both sides.

I teach a Harvard case study called "Changing Times at the NBA" to my MBA students at the Southern Methodist University (SMU) Cox School of Business. The case chronicles the league's image issues and struggles with player conduct. It is always interesting to hear the lively discussion around the case in class. It always comes down to the issue of how the NBA handles the Hip-Hop segment. The majority of my students are white, appreciate Hip-Hop for what it is, and unanimously agree that the NBA needs to find a way to embrace it.

I think the NBA has finally done just that, by no longer ignoring it and hoping it goes away. Similarly, to their credit, they have embraced the cultural trends that have led to the globalization of the sport and an influx of players from Europe and Asia. This positioning has given the NBA a brand platform and broadened its fan base.

The NBA has balanced the external contingencies beyond its control with internal contingencies it can control such as organizational vision and mission. Instead of ignoring the Hip-Hop gear and accessories that were becoming commonplace work attire, it worked with the NBA Players Association to implement a dress code to create a professional atmosphere. It worked.

As NBA great Charles Barkley says, when you make millions of dollars, there's nothing wrong with looking like it when you show up to work. In addition, the league took internal measures to ensure that the players had access to seasoned professionals in senior positions within key functions such as player development and communications including Steve Mills (who went on to serve as President of MSG and the New York Knicks), Shawn Bryant, Leah Wilcox, Chrysa Chin, Kevin Carr, and Terri Washington. These talented individuals were best in class and were also able to deftly bridge the Hip-Hop culture and NBA culture and get the players to buy into the league's initiatives and cause-based programs like NBA Cares.

As a result, the NBA began to change its tonality and defensive posture on the issue of the Hip-Hop generation in its quest for the next Jordan the association realized that it had to give these young men room to grow and market them collectively and on their own merits. The most recent NBA advertising campaigns have been brilliant in this sense. From "I Love This Game" to their "Amazing Happens Here" campaign and "There Can Only Be One" during the 2008 NBA Finals, it has taken the passion the players have for the game and turned the league into a canvas to express their artistic skills.

From a marketing standpoint, the NBA is selling an entertainment product inside of a basketball game. No one does it better. It has embraced the role that Hip-Hop music plays in that equation with the scripting of the in-game entertainment and arena experience. If you visit any NBA arena, even in homogenous markets like Boston, you'll find that Hip-Hop music is prevalent during the games.

In Detroit, the announcer brings Hip-Hop flavor to the introduction of the starting line-up and keeps the crowd engaged and entertained throughout the game, much as one expects from "Tango and Cash" at the infamous Rucker streetball tournament in Harlem.

The NBA has also aligned itself with corporate partners who want to grow market share by tapping into the lucrative urban market, particularly youth-driven brands like Sprite. Because of this, it is acceptable now for the athletes to be true to themselves without compromising potential corporate endorsements.

The well-crafted, manufactured image is no longer required for mainstream consumption. In fact, it pays to have a little edge, or street credibility. Just ask Kobe Bryant who is still searching to strike the right balance.

This notion is, perhaps, most prevalent for the sneaker brands that have long understood the significant role the urban consumer and Hip-Hop generation plays on their business and are no longer at odds with it. If you want to see how this plays out, watch the documentary *Through The Wire* which traces the journey of Stephon Marbury's cousin Sebastian Telfair from Lincoln High School on Coney Island to the NBA. At the press conference to announce their deal, Adidas marketing chief Kevin Wulff's primary talking point was Telfair's "street cred."

Perhaps, though, no one is better suited than LeBron James to be the chosen athlete to capitalize on this paradigm shift and represent the racial and global transcendence of the Hip-Hop generation. LeBron entered the league out of high school with the total package of performance, street credibility, charisma, and poise. All of this adds up to making him a global icon. His corporate partnerships have supported this notion. He is the first since Jordan to run the endorsement table, signing an unprecedented $90 million contract with Nike straight out of high school.

According to *Fortune* magazine, James raked in $25 million per year in endorsements in addition to his $13 million salary for the Cleveland Cavaliers in 2007. Overall, the magazine estimated King James' endorsement empire represented $170 million in sponsorship deals between Nike, Coca-Cola, Bubblicious, Cub Cadet, and MSN.

Much of this success can be attributed to agents Eric and Aaron Goodwin who facilitated his early deals. LeBron later jettisoned the Goodwin brothers and the traditional agent structure for a new business model that would be overseen by his own sports marketing company LRMR, comprised of James and three childhood friends. Given their lack of experience, the move was initially greeted with some skepticism by the NBA.

"I was nervous that LeBron was going to be represented by a group of his childhood friends," NBA deputy commissioner Adam Silver told *Fortune*. "Shortly after our first meeting, I had a sense of relief that LeBron was in good hands."

Their fears were allayed in part because James and his team smartly surrounded themselves with a brain trust of skilled accountants, lawyers, and advisors that include Warren Buffett and New York boutique investment bank Allen & Co. It remains to be seen, though, just how much James will capitalize on the opportunity as some questions remain surrounding his off-court personality and ability to connect with mainstream consumers à la Jordan, combined with some blows he suffered to his image among his once rock solid urban fan base.

One such blow was self-inflicted. I can recall during the Starbury launch many discussions with Stephon about how Nike's athletes would respond. Of course, we both knew it wouldn't be wise for them to speak out against the Starbury Movement because it was such a positive message, especially for the African-American community, and many of those same athletes were being called to task for not doing enough to give back to the community as previously discussed.

In fact, a few of the Nike athletes such as Carmelo Anthony, who came from tough, inner-city Baltimore, spoke out in support of what Stephon was doing at the outset. Then, King James spoke. Reporters asked him about his response to the Starbury affordable sneaker before going up against Marbury and the Knicks at Madison Square Garden in March of 2007.

His quote was "Me being with Nike, we hold our standards high." Surely he took the Nike PR department's talking points about innovation and performance and technology and veered off the script a bit. Stephon was ready. He typed his response to *New York Post* Knicks beat writer Marc Berman saying the Cavaliers guard "didn't do his homework." His response to LeBron. "I'd rather own than be owned." Even the *Cleveland Plain-Dealer* columnist questioned if he had forgotten his humble beginnings in Akron, Ohio, where many people were still struggling to get by.

A year later, James made history as the first black man to pose for *Vogue* **magazine.** But the image also stirred up controversy as some in the media decried the photo of **LeBron James and Brazilian model Gisele Bundchen** as perpetuating racial stereotypes. James struck what some saw as a gorilla-like pose, baring his teeth, with one hand dribbling the ball and the other around Bundchen's tiny waist, which conjured up images of King Kong and Fay Wray.

Clearly, James will be the most dominant player of his era, if not history, before he finishes. That said, his image and personality have yet to fully evolve and he could benefit from a PR strategist and advisor with requisite brand credentials and street smarts. Such a strategist could develop a brand positioning and image transcendence plan that add proper dimension to his personality and prevents cultural missteps such as the *Vogue* cover and Nike commercials. This is the base upon which his Nike fortunes, at least, rest. It may be no coincidence that his sneakers have yet to break through with this audience to Jordan standards. Surely everything King James does as heir to the Nike throne, will ultimately be measured against Air Jordan sales.

The emergence of And 1 and streetball

While the NBA was working through its challenges to get its stars, such as LeBron James, to align properly against a changing fan universe, an upstart brand named And 1 was trying to bring these heroes back down to the playground with an unknown galaxy of streetball stars with names like Skip To My Lou, Hot Sauce, AO, Main Event, and Headache. And 1 was founded in 1993 as a graduate school project partnership of Seth Berger, Jay Gilbert, and Abraham Osondu at the University of Pennsylvania. The founders were white kids with an affinity for Hip-Hop and urban culture. You'll recall from the profile of the Sub-Urban cipher that suburban kids are attracted to the realism of the urban experience in its most authentic form.

When it came to basketball in the early 1990s, nothing was more authentic than streetball. The founders were so enamored with the authenticity of streetball that they took the name "And 1," from what the playground ballers would yell when they were fouled in the act of shooting. Furthermore, the brand's early strategies included using slogans and trash talk on t-shirts such as "Pass. Save Yourself The Embarrassment." The beauty of this is they were using real-time urban vernacular and the Hip-Hop attitude that the ballers share. And 1 developed a niche, brought street ball to the masses, and created a cult following for its Mixtape Tour. It astutely exploited the natural marriage between sports, particularly basketball, and Hip-Hop music among the Core Urban consumers.

In its early stages of development, And 1 hired an underground Hip-Hop producer named "Free" to work with it and connect its brand to the Hip-Hop community.

Free is a great example of the Core Urban software developers mentioned earlier. Free brought innovation to And 1 by blending content from its summer Street Ball competitions with a soundtrack of unreleased songs from underground Hip-Hop artists with whom he had close ties. And 1 made the tapes available at athletic specialty retailers like Footaction, which could not keep them in stock. And 1 was riding the wave of its Mixtape Tour success when it contacted me in the summer of 2001 because it wanted to take the Tour to the next level. At the time, the plan was to tour four cities that would provide content for that year's Mixtape.

I was always impressed by And 1's brand, although it never totally factored into our competitive set at Nike, but that would soon change. I suggested to And 1's marketing team that we look at the Mixtape Tour players like the stars of the Negro Leagues. These players had become just as popular as the NBA athletes because they were from the same environment. While NBA players bought fancy cribs in the suburbs, the streetballers still lived around the way.

I remember being in the Bronx, New York, with "Shane The Dribbling Machine" during the And 1 Mixtape Tour and seeing the kids running out of the housing projects to greet him. It reminded me of Richard Pryor and the movie *Bingo Long and the All-Stars.*

For this reason, I convinced And 1 to create a tour bus and take the

players on a nationwide tour with impromptu stops at radio stations, retail stores, barber shops, and other consumer touch points. The result was incredible.

Remember what I said about Core Urban consumers being content creators. Well, you can imagine how much great footage was created from the tour. This fact wasn't lost on ESPN who came along for the ride and eventually created *Streetball,* a series on ESPN2 devoted to the And 1 Mixtape Tour.

And 1 benefited from the urban culture life cycle and evolution in the way that Core Urban trends and innovations eventually reach the mainstream. An international tour soon followed as did its first Caucasian player, The Professor. The Professor did for streetball what Eminem did for Hip-Hop music. He studied the styles of the Core Urban streetballers and added his own suburban twist.

This mainstream growth of streetball also caught the attention of other brands looking to reach the Hip-Hop audience. One was Mountain Dew, which signed on as a sponsor of the tour and heavily promoted the athletes as comic book characters in its advertising. While the sponsorship dollars surely boosted the P&L for And 1, the end of the life cycle for the brand and streetball came once it was fully mainstream and commercialized and departed from its authentic, grass roots.

The 1990s also saw the Hip-Hop generation innovate an entire apparel category and breathe life into a sports product that was literally sitting on the shelf. It took a savvy sales associate to convince the owner of Mitchell & Ness, a Philadelphia retailer, to allow him to seed some of the store's NBA legend sports jerseys with rappers to create demand for the jerseys which were, essentially, collecting dust.

"Throwback" jerseys bearing the names of Julius Erving and Jerry West eventually became ubiquitous in Hip-Hop videos and inner cities across America and spawned additional brands developing authentic, throwback jerseys in a variety of colors and offerings boosting sales for athletic specialty chains like Foot Locker. Once again demonstrating his EF Hutton effect on the Hip-Hop generation, Jay-Z brought sales of the throwback jerseys to a screeching halt when he declared in one of his songs he was eschewing the popular jerseys in favor of a more mature style. Almost instantaneously, as in the case of Cristal, Hip-Hoppers retired the legendary jerseys back to the shelf.

The Williams sisters transform tennis

The Hip-Hop generation's impact on basketball was to be expected. However, given the cultural and social trends that fueled participation, no one could have predicted that African Americans would transform the establishment sports of tennis and golf—for many years elitist sports that did not accept African Americans. Althea Gibson and Arthur Ashe were the standard bearers in tennis that paved the way for modern African-American participation and players such as Zina Garrison, who achieved great success on the women's USTA circuit. However, two sisters named Venus and Serena would change the sport of tennis forever.

Like their Hip-Hop generation peers, they did it with their skills as well as their self-expression and creativity. Their canvas was not the private country club but the public courts where their father Richard coached them. The stodgy tennis community did not know how to react to the sisters who sported braids and beads and hailed from Compton, California, made infamous by the controversial group N.W.A.

While they were pulverizing their opponents on the court, the endorsements failed to keep pace off the court with the exception of a few sponsors, including Reebok, Wilson, Puma, and Wrigley's Doublemint. At Edelman PR in 2001, my team was brought in to help Wrigley's maximize its partnership with the Williams sisters, as part of its strategy to reach the urban market, which over-indexed on Wrigley's Doublemint. The green Doublemint packs were ubiquitous and the gum of choice in the urban market. There was nothing more detrimental to one's urban self-image than bad breath and Doublemint did the trick.

We scheduled a press announcement during the Sony Ericsson tournament in Key Biscayne, Florida, March 22, 2001. During this time, Venus and Serena were almost unfairly dominating the sport. In fact, they would go on to meet in the four consecutive Grand Slam finals in 2001–2002 and stayed No.1 and No. 2 in the rankings for a year.

This prompted the media and other players to accuse them of playing only in selected tournaments, especially when pitted against one another. This sentiment boiled over the weekend prior during the tournament at Indian Wells, California, when Venus pulled out of the semifinal against Serena at the last minute due to injury. The girls were booed. Their father, Richard Williams, claimed the reaction was racially motivated and alleged that racial epithets were hurled at them as well.

With this as a backdrop to the Wrigley's announcement, we decided to conduct the press conference via telephone to inoculate Venus & Serena from a cynical media. I set the stage for the call telling the reporters that we were there to announce an exciting new partnership between two household names, Wrigley's Doublemint and the Williams sisters. It celebrated their shared values of being distinctively different and we would like to keep the focus on the partnership between the Williams sisters and Wrigley's.

A review of the transcript revealed it didn't take long, the third reporter to be exact, for questions to be raised about the girls' desire to compete against each other.

> **Q:** Do you as competitors fear playing each other? How difficult is it for you to play each other?

> **Erin Patton:** Sir, we'd like to keep the questions focused to this particular announcement today. Next call.

> **Q:** This is for both of the sisters. I know you would prefer to talk about other things. But considering all of the controversy of recent days, if you just have any message for your fans that we could relay for you regarding that controversy.

> **Erin Patton:** Next question, please.

> Venus passed a note to me that she wished to address that particular reporter from the *Washington Post* and proceeded to squash the issue.

Venus Williams: Really, I just want to say to all my fans, everyone watching, really just not believe everything that you read. And Serena and I, we're really great competitors. We're fierce competitors. We really have no fear of playing each other. We've done it on five occasions already including two Grand Slams, and we really are just both looking forward to playing this week.

I learned from being around them that Venus is the designated spokesperson for the siblings. The announcement was a success and Venus made it to the final. During the tournament, I had the pleasure of meeting Larry Bailey who handled the Williams sisters' finances. I mentioned to Larry that I wanted to work with Venus and Serena and help them navigate the troubled PR waters and maximize their marketability.

He suggested I contact their attorney Kevin Davis in Seattle. I sent an email to Keven and outlined some of my thoughts on ways I thought I could help the team. Keven was responsible for the record-setting deal Venus signed with Reebok and had a reputation as a master negotiator. Shortly after I left Edelman to start my firm, I received an RFP from Keven for the girls' publicist search. I put together a great package and sent it off feeling confident I would get it, especially after proving my mettle with the girls through the Wrigley's announcement and Indian Wells controversy.

Unfortunately, there are times when gender can work against men in sports. In this case, having been nurtured by an inner-circle and brain trust of men who protected their interests and careers with great care, they opted for female publicists, which I fully understood though I was disappointed.

One thing I've learned in the sports business is that you have to continue to mine your relationships, and staying top of mind is a daily requirement. I did just that with Keven and eventually got the call from him to help out with brand development and partnership strategies for Venus and her Reebok relationship that had stalled. Serena had just joined Nike from Puma and I could be of assistance to her as well.

I worked closely with Keven and Isha Price, Venus and Serena's sister, on positioning and marketing strategies. I also spoke to Venus and Serena at length regarding their views on how their partners should best leverage their images. Venus, like her name, was truly universal and had transcended all boundaries. She was eccentric in her style and had begun fashion design school and started an interior design company so she brought credibility to Reebok, which they never fully capitalized on.

Race was never an issue for either of the Williams sisters. They handled the subject with grace and an elevated consciousness and self-awareness that resulted from their global experiences and exposure that was beyond just black and white. I admired them greatly for that. This was especially true of Venus. I titled her brand plan "No Boundaries" which captured her completely from her style to her mainstream appeal.

Serena embodied the very icon and word "Nike" represented which was the Greek goddess of victory. Serena was striking, powerful, and had a killer instinct. I even suggested in the plan that my former Nike colleagues build its Nike Goddess line around Serena. I also worked with Keven on the Wilson deal for Venus and Serena. Shortly after the launch of Starbury in the fall of 2006, I approached Venus' agent Carlos Fleming from IMG about having Venus do a line for Steve & Barry's after learning her deal was up with Reebok.

While he was aware the retailer was making noise with Starbury, he had legitimate concerns about how the value channel positioning would compromise Venus' plans to play at the top of the pyramid and penetrate other mass-market channels such as department stores. I told Carlos I thought it would actually demonstrate her ability to move product to the masses, which would establish a positive track record and bode well for her in other channels down the road.

I mentioned that Reebok had failed to capitalize on Venus' creative instincts and design credibility. This created the opening for me to introduce Venus to Steve & Barry's with a major selling point for the partnership being her designer credibility. The retailer would allow Venus to be totally involved in the design and development of her line and push the fashion envelope, which was a radical departure from Reebok.

We scheduled a visit for **Venus** to the Manhattan Mall store. She was intrigued by the notion of having uninhibited creative license and was also impressed by the quality of the merchandise. As we walked the store, she was calling out fabrics. Her fashion style is also distinct so it was not a stretch for her to marry fashion-forward styles with Steve & Barry's affordability.

While a piece of the brand narrative touched upon her background growing up in Compton, unlike Starbury, we grounded **Venus Williams' EleVen brand** positioning in her designer credibility as a student of fashion. During the initial product and marketing review, we wrestled with the strategic decision whether to launch during the U.S. Open later that fall or wait for the holiday season.

The consensus was that the U.S. Open was the "Super Bowl" of tennis and a window we couldn't miss. Venus had seen her rankings slip that year but was clearly energized by the launch of her line and was in excellent condition. In June, Venus won her fourth Wimbledon title to set the stage for the soft launch during the U.S. Open, She repeated the feat in 2008 for a back-to-back and fifth Wimbledon championship, this time emerging victorious over younger sister Serena. I watched proudly with my sons as Venus held up the Wimbledon trophy, sporting the EleVen brand. Game, set, match.

CHAPTER 9

Corporate America &

Whenever my MBA students ask me about business books I suggest, one that is always on my short list is *The Innovator's Dilemma* by Clayton Christensen. Because I'm based in Dallas, a hotbed for technology, the book always resonates.

The author's main theme is that established corporations are not good at what he calls "disruptive technologies," which are machines or techniques that are inadequate in some ways, yet, which have great future potential.

Corporations often fail to invest in disruptive technologies because the market doesn't exist or they do not recognize the potential market. As Christensen writes, "in the battle for development resources, projects targeted at the explicit needs of current customers or at the needs of existing users that a supplier has not yet been able to reach will always win over proposals to develop products for markets that do not exist."

Instead, managers at established companies are trained to recognize and aggressively invest in what Christensen calls "sustaining technologies" and innovations in order to keep pace with the competition. A sustaining technology is usually more sophisticated than the original version but also takes more expertise to manufacture and requires more expensive production lines.

In the end, sustaining innovation makes products more appealing to existing customers by improving the state-of-the-art in ways everyone can appreciate. The end product in this case may be based on different physical principles but it is functionally equivalent and it fills the same customer needs. Therein lies the problem.

One might argue that sustaining technologies are not true innovations at all. While they appear safer and less risky, sustaining technologies are less profitable than disruptive technologies that require less R&D investment. According to Christensen's research, "the firms that led in launching disruptive products logged a cumulative total of $62 billion dollars in revenues between 1976 and 1994. Those that followed into the market later, after those markets had been established, logged only $3.3 billion on total revenue."

Firms that sought growth by entering small, emerging markets logged 20 times the revenues of the firms pursuing growth in larger, established markets.

So, where am I going with this?

Christensen's hypothesis on disruptive and sustaining technologies is powerful and also analogous to what I call corporate America's Hip-Hop Innovator's Dilemma.

Let's take an example from an earlier chapter. Remember, the Hpnotiq Incredible Hulk drink I mentioned earlier? This "disruptive innovation" came about by an urban bartender or "mixologist" who observed that the urban males in the club would not drink the blue drink because it appeared too fruity and feminine.

He mixed Hpnotiq with Hennessy and the rest is history. He altered both the form and function of the product and created a new flavor. No R&D necessary. It all transpired in the clinical laboratory of the human experience, where the greatest disruptions originate, with one innovator creatively recognizing the opportunity to fulfill the needs of a niche audience.

In this case, the niches were the Contemporary Urban and Organic Urban segments, comprised of music industry executives and young professionals who gathered weekly at P. Diddy's Justin's Restaurant in New York to network, socialize, and enjoy the fruits of their upwardly mobile lifestyle. When they approached the bar, they came in search of what was new and the bartender, a member of the Hip-Hop generation himself, knew this.

Meanwhile, back in the far away labs, the product developers and those charged with developing new "technologies" for the liquor companies were surely oblivious to this niche audience and unaware of such disruptions. They were only looking for ways to improve upon their original versions and investing considerably in R&D in the process.

Imagine if Absolut, which had the first-mover advantage with this audience, had recognized the Hip-Hop generation's disruptive innovations within the spirits category in the 1990s and invested in product development that appealed to this niche audience's preferences for flavored drinks. Imagine if Absolut had recognized their move toward taste refinement and brown liquors instead of merely investing in technologies to keep pace with the competition. It would have profited tremendously and potentially thwarted the rise of competitors such as Hpnotiq, which is vodka-based and mixed with fruits and cognac.

Fortunately for Hpnotiq, the Incredible Hulk innovation came from the "bottom-up" within its brand experience and grass roots activity to engage urban consumers with on-premise trial. Many brands simply get lucky this way because the Hip-Hop generation constantly innovates around products and brands as they seek enhanced experiences.

In the end, these large brands are left wondering how this brand insurgency is happening but refuse to act upon it, even wishing it away in the face of their "core customer." This is especially true among luxury and premium brands that are brand purists and have a centuries-old customer base in many cases. They have very little understanding of the modern, high-end urban market segment. Their perspectives are clouded by stereotypes that are perpetuated in the media and the narrow lens through which they view the urban lifestyle, such as music videos that make this phenomenon somewhat self-perpetuating.

It is what led fashion house Fendi to make disparaging remarks years ago when rappers like Lil' Kim and Foxy Brown gravitated toward its designer bags and prompted the Cristal executive to make the condescending comment I mentioned earlier that offended Jay-Z.

Instead of embracing this niche audience and the positive, disruptive innovation the Hip-Hop generation brought to lifestyle celebration occasions that the brand could have fully leveraged, the Cristal executive balked.

While I'm not sure how much Hpnotiq subsequently leveraged the window of opportunity to invest further in the Hip-Hop generation and urban consumer's potential for future disruptive innovations, the fact that the brand eventually cooled is a good indication that it failed to do so.

Not knowing the origins of the disruptive technology, and consciously or unconsciously blocking the internal change agents seeking to push innovation up through layers of bureaucracy based on what these new customers value, Hpnotiq likely focused the majority of its investment on its sustaining technologies and "core customer."

As such, it became content with milking the unexpected profits derived from urban consumers and Hip-Hop, making little investment in this emerging market while hoping these staunchly loyal consumers would maintain their brand affinity.

This *is* the crux of corporate America's Hip-Hop generation dilemma. In meetings, on conference calls, and behind closed doors, the discussion goes something like this:

- How much do we invest in this niche audience?
- What is the return on investment?
- Whose budget does it come out of?
- We don't want to chase trends do we?
- What about our core customers?
- How big is the market?
- Won't they spend with us anyway?

This loop continues. Fear of the unknown. Many have accurately called this the paralysis of analysis.

These large organizations ultimately defer to what they know best—the market that most resembles them and their experiences because it is too far of a leap to imagine a fundamental shift to whom and how they market. Contrary to what many allege as bias, the only bias I attribute this to is a lack of exposure. It is difficult to understand these dynamics that operate far beneath the surface-level observation. This lack of understanding is further exacerbated when you are so far removed from the user experience.

This is what prompted the 7 Ciphers segmentation framework. The framework allows companies to identify specific, niche audiences within the emerging urban market to ensure precise, efficient marketing, ROI, and profit maximization. It also reveals their insights into brand preferences, product attributes, and potential disruptive innovations. For Motorola and the Two-Way Pager, it was the Contemporary Urban cipher. For Coors Light, it was the Alternative Urban cipher and so on.

As established companies overlook the market potential and growth afforded by disruptive technologies and innovations emanating from emerging niche markets and segments, the forces of disruption that can invade the mainstream constantly threaten their future survival. That's why it is so important to have a diverse work force. This is the business case.

Venus Williams' EleVen line and Starbury are examples of disruptions that invaded the mainstream and completely took the industry off-guard and put the larger manufacturers in a position to wait and see how quickly the innovation moved as they were in no position to replicate it.

As Christensen outlines in his book, large companies were unable to duplicate the affordable sneaker model because "what goes up, can't go back down." Once a company sells to the high-end market, it cannot easily back down and introduce cheaper, mass market models. In the case of Steve & Barry's, the major brands were never really faced with this dilemma beyond the initial launch because the retailer was not able to increase the value perception of its private label brands by investing in further disruptive innovation and technologies.

For example, had Steve & Barry's invested in product designers representing the Hip-Hop generation or poached them from urban brands, particularly apparel, instead of the mainstream brands from which it hired designers, the insurgency could have continued.

Also, the company could have innovated with a "Big & Tall" line for Ben Wallace of the Chicago Bulls that would have given it ownership of an untapped niche. Finally, the retailer could have extended its model into doing deals with Hip-Hop artists to make CDs affordable and focused part of its growth strategy and footprint on urban retail. Such efforts would have posed a more significant dilemma for Nike, Reebok, and Adidas.

Instead, the once upstart innovative company shied away from investing against the urban target and began to operate from the top down like its larger competitors such as the Gap. Gap, meanwhile, suffered at the hands of specialty retailers such as Abercrombie & Fitch and Urban Outfitters that grew out of the Sub-Urban cipher's disruptive innovation.

Golden rules for marketing to the Hip-Hop generation

How does an organization solve this Hip-Hop Innovator's Dilemma?

Here are my cardinal rules for maximizing the influence of the Hip-Hop generation and urban consumers for the multitude of brands that face this dilemma.

Rule #1: Keep in Touch

During a cultural immersion I participated in for Coors Brewing Company, I wrote three words on the easel before dismissing my breakout group. Keep in touch. I wasn't talking about me, though. I was talking about the consumer touch points. Large organizations and management must find ways to stay connected to the relevant touch points for the urban consumer and have the courage to invest significantly in this emerging general market once disruptive innovations present themselves.

It begins with human capital investment. In addition to placing diverse talent within the marketing ranks, companies need to make a concerted diversity recruitment effort in the areas of product design and development or create a process that fosters an exchange between urban innovators and the R&D function. The process should bring their rich insights into the organization and allow them to impact product development.

HIP-HOP QUOTABLE

Why they didn't make the CL6 with a clutch.
JADAKISS, "WHY?"

I developed such a concept for Motorola by establishing a new product advisory board comprised of highly mobile types within the sports and entertainment industries. General Motors and Cadillac have also been very successful at this.

Recognizing the strong affinity the Hip-Hop generation was demonstrating for the Escalade through after-market customization, Cadillac provided interactive focus group settings and other feedback mechanisms for the urban consumer to give input on product design, features, and benefits so the vehicles would come equipped standard with some of these very features.

The failure by Lincoln-Mercury to recognize the disruptive innovation occurring within the urban automotive sub-culture allowed Escalade to steal market share from Lincoln Navigator which had the first-mover advantage as the luxury SUV-of-choice among the ballers.

To maximize the effectiveness of such a strategy, these individuals must be paid for their expertise and an expert with an intimate understanding of the culture should take the lead role in identifying them and solidifying their trust. Many brands have attempted to glean insights or endorsements from Hip-Hop artists and other urban innovators and opinion leaders on the cheap. They recognize it a mile away.

On the creative side, advertising agencies have to look around during the meetings and ask themselves if they are a true reflection of the marketplace. This is why the Madison Avenue diversity project has to be more than symbolic. If an advertising agency doesn't demonstrate a sustained commitment, clients need to find one that will because it is to their benefit to do so. By integrating executives from the Hip-Hop generation into senior-level account management and creative positions, all relevant touch points will be met.

Furthermore, and perhaps most importantly, these individuals will serve as filters for the organization and prevent stereotypes and other offenses that Pepper Miller called the "Joe The Boxer" moment in her book, *What's Black About It?* The ad features an underwear-clad African American prancing about in apparent glee. I'm sure it was hilarious in the creative review, but it was offensive. This could have been avoided if the creative team at that agency had the Hip-Hop generation filter present.

Rule #2: Learn What Urban Customers Value

While Hip-Hop has had an enormous influence on the urban mindset and popular culture, urban consumers value more than just the music and Hip-Hop lifestyle. There are many sources of inspiration and a rich set of experiences within the culture that lead to emotional and rational decisions and behavior.

I mentioned this previously during the Starbury case study but it bears mentioning again. Know thy customer. Too often, organizations don't calibrate properly against the appropriate target or segment(s) within the urban market from the outset. As a result, strategy and creative are off, ROI and measurement fails. Market research has to be a priority but not strictly in the traditional sense. My agency has developed an innovative, ethnographic approach to qualitative research. We coordinate real-world immersions where product designers and developers come in contact with innovators in the real-time urban consumer laboratory. It's priceless.

Organizations, guided by experts, have to make this type of concerted effort toward understanding what urban consumers value and how that differs from other market segments. In the case of Steve & Barry's, urban consumers didn't so much value the innovation in the $15 price for the Starbury sneaker as much as they did the innovation behind Stephon Marbury's vision and the emotional context of the Starbury Movement. Finally an NBA athlete and celebrity was willing to stand up for them and do something different to eliminate the pressure kids felt. Without us bringing that perspective to the meeting, the retailer had its sights set firmly on the moms in Iowa who valued price and "jaw-dropping prices," which would have never succeeded in bringing about the industry disruption we created from the bottom up.

When taking this market-based approach, it may turn out that the urban market is the general market for some brands. When it appears this is the case, embrace it. As Hip-Hop's Generation X matures, luxury brands should be proactively looking for ways to align against this target.

Rule #3: Avoid One-Night Brand Stands

While the Hip-Hop generation is staunchly loyal, they also recognize when a brand is committed or merely feigning it for their affection. Marketing to this audience has to be a sustained commitment over time. The tendency for most large brands has been to go after it one year and pull back investment the next. These consumers recognize when brands are "in it to win it" and will support those brands over the long haul. The Hip-Hop generation is constantly reinventing itself so a sustained effort is necessary to ensure that a brand is running the most recent "urban culture software" on its operating system.

Rule #4: Everything That Counts Can't Be Counted

The question invariably becomes, "How does one measure the effect of the Hip-Hop generation?" While ROI is extremely important, and traditional measurement metrics should be built into urban marketing campaigns, it is also important to recognize that everything that counts can't be counted when it comes to the Hip-Hop generation.

For years, product and brand mentions and product placement within Hip-Hop music and videos were commonplace and did correlate to consumer behavior.

In many respects, Adidas' brand position in the urban market can be attributed to this day to Run-DMC's classic song "My Adidas."

When I worked at Nike, I often knew how successful the brand was based on the number of product mentions I heard in songs and saw in videos. In fact, this became a concerted effort and part of my marketing strategy. I made sure that my colleague Nekeda Newell who was in the Hollywood Promo group for Nike was a key part of my team as we introduced new Jordan product. Nekeda had great relationships with the artists and we made sure they got the latest product first.

San Francisco-based pop culture strategy firm Agenda began tracking these product and brand mentions in Hip-Hop music with its "American Brandstand" report in 2003. The report tallied the number of mentions or gross impressions rappers delivered for certain brands throughout the year. This was free publicity that reinforces Christensen's theory on the cost of disruptive technologies being much cheaper per unit, or CPM (cost per thousand) in this case.

In a 2005 interview with *Brandweek,* Agenda's founder Lucien James accurately pinpointed the implications of this "bottom up" form of disruptive innovation and data by the Hip-Hop generation on corporate America.

"One of the things it does is it demonstrates which brands have captured the public imagination. Successful brands can't be perfectly created back at the headquarters. Brands have a life of their own in pop culture. American Brandstand reflects how brands are being interpreted by pop culture, especially Hip-Hop culture, which will be incredibly important to watch as it becomes more global."

This product and brand integration has to be organic, though, to be successful. McDonald's found this out in 2005 when it announced that it would be paying Hip-Hop artists to mention the Big Mac in their songs. It was a short-lived strategy.

Rule #5: Skate Toward the Puck

As the Hip-Hop generation has evolved, transcended the globe, and influenced brands, pop culture, and sports in the process, it has arrived at a crossroads and is now poised to lead the way into the future. The Millennials will write the future chapter. They have been shaped and influenced by the sheer innovation of the Hip-Hop generation, which has fueled new paradigms, open-source systems, and user-generated content and brands. The Hip-Hop generation's political awareness is also producing a new generation of leaders and interest in the political process.

Race will become less of a factor and psychographic segmentation will be the key for brands to unlock the future Hip-Hop generation. While crass commercialism and a lack of creativity has prompted many from within the culture to begin to write Hip-Hop's eulogy, Hip-Hop music and culture will surely reinvent itself. It's simply in the DNA. The brands that will be successful will be those who are able to recognize the future paradigm and skate toward where the puck is going, not simply where it is at the moment.

The Hip-Hop generation also faces a sobering dilemma. When discussing the plight facing urban consumers, particularly the Hip-Hop culture-conscious rapper Mos Def responded by saying blacks suffer from "terminal consumerism."

If this country is in recession, one sure can't tell by the spending habits of urban consumers. From clothing to cars and gadgets to jewels, urban consumers simply have to have it, literally, at all costs. In fact, it appears that when the going gets tough, urban consumers really get going with their spending. While consumers in the general market are currently tightening their purse strings in response to a soft U.S. economy, urban consumers remain quite loose in their spending.

There are a few factors that account for this: In addition to the aforementioned obsession with material objects as status symbols which is exacerbated by the bombardment of marketing messages and specific products designed to manipulate a consumer-driven mentality, urban consumers have been conditioned to develop consistent spending habits and buying patterns in spite of living in a constant recession mode.

In other words, the economic belt for urban consumers is always tight so buying habits don't really change when the economy as a whole tightens another notch or two. As such, urban consumers are positioned to be the driving forces for companies that want to maintain brand momentum and stimulate growth in many key industries. The smartest brands are recognizing this and have adjusted their marketing spend with urban consumers to grow the pie in a saturated mainstream market.

So, where is all of this going? Just as he so eloquently stated the problem, I'll leave the answer to Mos Def.

> Listen . . . people be askin me all the time
> "Yo Mos, what's getting ready to happen with Hip-Hop?"
> (Where do you think Hip-Hop is goin?)
> I tell'em. "You know what's gonna happen with Hip-Hop?
> Whatever's happening with us"
> If we smoked out, Hip-Hop is gonna be smoked out
> If we doin alright, Hip-Hop is gonna be doin alright
> People talk about Hip-Hop like it's some giant livin in the hillside
> Comin down to visit the townspeople
> We are Hip-Hop
> Me, you, everybody, we are Hip-Hop
> So Hip-Hop is goin where we goin
> So the next time you ask yourself where Hip-Hop is goin
> Ask yourself . . . where am I goin? How am I doin?
>
> **MOS DEF, "FEAR NOT OF MAN"**

Yes, that's why I love Hip-Hop. Just as it did that day in 1987 sitting in my calculus class, it always reminds me of who I am, how I'm doing and, most importantly, where I'm going.

ERIN PATTON is widely regarded as one of the nation's foremost experts on branding, sports marketing and Hip-Hop culture. Under his leadership, The Mastermind Group (TMG) emerged as a recognized leader for brand management and groundbreaking strategic partnerships, providing counsel to an exclusive roster of Fortune 500 brands and pop culture icons.

Patton has been widely acclaimed for "cracking the code on the urban market" with his breakthrough 7 Ciphers™ segmentation study that attracted flagship sponsors including Pepsi and The Brookings Institution. He has also been instrumental in the most notable footwear product launches in recent memory. During his tenure with Nike, Inc, he served as the original architect for the Jordan brand, engineering its successful launch in 1997. He later spearheaded NBA-star Stephon Marbury's award-winning Starbury brand launch that revolutionized the sneaker industry and earned launch of the year honors from *Footwear News* and *Advertising Age* in 2006.

Patton has been recognized with awards from distinguished organizations including the coveted Edison Award from the American Marketing Association, United Nations Honorable Mention, International Public Relations Association, The Network Journal's "Forty Under

Forty Award" and the Innovator Award from the Advertising Research Foundation (ARF).

Gifted as a dynamic public speaker with extraordinary communication skills, Patton is sought as a speaker for conferences, workshops, universities and corporations. He has also appeared as an expert on ESPN, CNN, VH1, and BET and been quoted in *USA Today, Time, Inc., BusinessWeek, Wall Street Journal and Fortune.*

As a staunch advocate for higher education, Patton serves as Adjunct Professor of Sports Marketing in the Cox School of Business at Southern Methodist University (SMU) where he also directs its Sports Management Consortium targeting front-office executives and athletes with innovative executive education programs.

As a civic leader, Patton devotes his time, talent and treasure to various national non-profit organizations and causes, including KaBOOM!, which builds playgrounds in underserved areas, and Positive Coaching Alliance (PCA), which uses sports to teach life lessons and character development. He is also a board member of the Texas Leadership Forum, SMU Athletic Forum, and Hispanic Youth Symposium, a program of the Hispanic College Fund.

Patton is a graduate of Northwestern University in Evanston, Illinois. He earned his MBA from the SMU Cox School of Business in Dallas. He currently resides in Frisco, Texas, with his wife Nicole and two young sons.